Edgar Cayce and *The Urantia Book*

READER REVIEWS

"Love, Love, Love Edgar Cayce! If you have read the Urantia book then you must read Edgar Cayce and the Urantia book. Karen Pressler & John Bunker have put extensive hours of research into their claims regarding this book and hands down is a must read! I could not put it down, I was completely spellbound until the end!"

Shana
Amazon review

"Your pdf exceeded any expectations I thought your work would bring. It was extremely easy to understand and well written. I commend you for your efforts. I read it in one sitting because I could not put it down."

Tyson,
Seattle, WA

"Since your theory is well-supported by your research and since any other information about the sleeping subject is very limited, your "Edgar Cayce and the Urantia Book" should be included in any search for the identity of that mysterious assistant to the Urantia revelation."

Rod
Amazon review

"The material (Book) was excellent and the logic and investigation very well done. I would recommend the read, regardless of your belief."

Seumas
Amazon review

EDGAR CAYCE

AND

THE URANTIA BOOK

Third Edition

John M. Bunker
Karen L. Pressler

Edgar Cayce and *The Urantia Book*
Copyright ©1999, 2009, 2017 by John M. Bunker

ISBN   978-0988500181

Questions regarding this book can be addressed to the author:

John M. Bunker
8829 Heffelfinger Rd.
Churubusco, IN 46723

johnb@protelmarketing.com (e-mail)
http://www.edgarcayceandtheurantiabook.com/ (web page)

Acknowledgments

Thank you to all of the following people, without whose help the original book would not have been possible.

Mike Brewer
Edgar Evans Cayce
Meredith Sprunger
David Kruse
Matthew Block
D. D. Cayce
Charles 'Bud' Bromley
Stuart Dean
Douglas Bull
Debbie Brown
Dr. Vonne Meussling

Table of Contents

COMMENTS BY EDGAR EVANS CAYCE XI
COMMENTS BY MEREDITH J. SPRUNGER XIII
COMMENTS BY MARTIN GARDNER... XIV
KAREN'S INTRODUCTION.. XVI
JOHN'S INTRODUCTION TO THE SECOND EDITION............................. XXI
PREFACE XXIII

PART I: OVERVIEW AND HISTORICAL FACTS 3

   1. INTRODUCTION 3
     Nola Smith 6
   2. THE SIGNIFICANCE OF LANGUAGE.. 11
   3. MISSING CAYCE READINGS 18
   4. THE EFFECTS OF SECRECY 20
     Professional Ethics and Confidentiality 20
     The Threat of the American Medical Association 20
   5. USE OF EXISTING TEXTS 24
   6. CAYCE IN CHICAGO 27
   7. THE STOCK MARKET CONNECTION 30
   8. HISTORICAL POINTS OF INTEREST.. 31
     Ancient Mesopotamian Cities.. 31
     The Three Concentric Circles.. 31

PART II. THE PEOPLE INVOLVED 35

   1. INTRODUCTION 37
     People Involved with Sadler and Cayce 38
   2. WILLIAM S. SADLER 41
   3. SADLER WRITES ABOUT THE SLEEPING SUBJECT............................. 44
     Appendix of The Mind at Mischief... 46
   4. WHEN DID SADLER BECOME INVOLVED WITH CAYCE?.................. 61
     Ecce Quam Bonum 61
     Three Different Accounts of the 1906 Meeting........................... 62
     The Private E.Q.B. Files.. 64
     The Size of the E.Q.B. Meetings 64
   5. THE HEARSTS, THE FIELDS, AND THE KELLOGGS.............................. 67
   6. HARRY LOOSE AND HAROLD SHERMAN 71
   7. SHERMAN AND CAYCE.. 79
   8. SHERMAN AND WILKINS 81
   9. SIR HUBERT WILKINS - THE MISSING LINK 83
   10. THE TWO MAGICIANS 89
   11. THE PUBLICATIONS... 94

PART III: STORIES CONCERNING *THE URANTIA BOOK* **97**

1. REMARKS ABOUT DR. SADLER'S PAPERS 99
   History of the Urantia Movement *100*
   Contact Activities Preceding the Urantia Papers *101*
   How the Urantia Papers Started *104*
   How the Forum Started *106*
   Introduction of the Forum to the "Contacts" *107*
   The Forum Begins to Ask Questions *109*
   The Forum Becomes a Closed Group *113*
   Receiving the Completed Papers *117*
   Reason for Silence Respecting Details of the Origin of The Urantia
   Book *119*
   How We Got the Urantia Papers *122*
2. THE BILL SADLER, JR. TAPE *125*
3. OTHER STORIES CONCERNING *THE URANTIA BOOK* *144*
   Humor *144*
   Story Concerning a Safety Deposit Box *144*
   Stories of the Identity of the Contact Person *145*

PART IV: FINAL COMMENTS **147**

1. THE COMMUNICATIONS *149*
   Mandate Limiting Revealed Knowledge *149*
   Development of Terms *150*
   Living and Deceased Mortal Minds Were Sources of Information
   ....*151*
2. OTHER SIMILARITIES REGARDING CAYCE AND *THE URANTIA BOOK*
   ....*153*
   Closing Statement *163*

PART V: APPENDICES **165**

APPENDIX A: DR. SADLER'S PAPERS *167*
   HISTORY OF THE URANTIA MOVEMENT *167*
   CONTACT ACTIVITIES PRECEDING THE URANTIA PAPERS
   ....*167*
   HOW THE URANTIA PAPERS STARTED *170*
   HOW THE FORUM STARTED *171*
   INTRODUCTION OF THE FORUM TO THE "CONTACTS" *171*
   THE FORUM BEGINS TO ASK QUESTIONS *172*
   THE FORUM BECOMES A CLOSED GROUP *173*
   THE FIRST URANTIA PAPERS *174*
   RECEIVING THE COMPLETED PAPERS *174*
   THE DELAY IN RECEIVING THE JESUS PAPERS *174*

REASON FOR SILENCE RESPECTING DETAILS OF THE
ORIGIN OF THE URANTIA BOOK 175
HOW WE GOT THE URANTIA PAPERS 176
HOW WE DID NOT GET THE URANTIA BOOK 179
FUNCTIONING OF THE CONTACT COMMISSIONERS 180
THE SEVENTY 181
THE PUBLICATION MANDATE 181
THE URANTIA FOUNDATION 182
THE URANTIA BROTHERHOOD 183
PREAMBLE 184
ACTIVITIES OF URANTIA BROTHERHOOD 185
DISTRIBUTION OF THE URANTIA BOOK 186
URANTIA BROTHERHOOD CORPORATION 187
THE URANTIA BROTHERHOOD SCHOOL 187
APPENDIX B: DR. WILLIAM S. SADLER 190
APPENDIX C: DATES CAYCE WAS IN CHICAGO 193
APPENDIX D: CAYCE-URANTIA TIMELINE 196
APPENDIX E: ANCIENT MESOPOTAMIAN CITIES 220
APPENDIX F: WORDS AND IDEAS FROM THE PRINCIPLES OF NATURE,
HER DIVINE REVELATIONS, AND A VOICE TO MANKIND 222
APPENDIX G: THE SEALED URANTIA ARCHIVES 224
APPENDIX H: FINDING DR. VONNE MEUSSLING 226
BIBLIOGRAPHY 229
INDEX 233

Comments by Edgar Evans Cayce

I have read *Edgar Cayce and The Urantia Book*. John Bunker has done extensive research examining the possibility that there may have been some connection between Edgar Cayce and this book. Coupled with the similarities unearthed by John's work is the fact that there were not that many individuals giving psychic readings during the time the book was written. Who else could it have been?

Standing against the evidence John has produced is:

❑ Nowhere in the Cayce readings is there any mention of the hierarchy of angels which fills Urantia.

❑ *The Urantia Book* does not support the theory of reincarnation, so prevalent in the life readings given by Edgar Cayce.

Though Cayce did not remember anything he said in his readings, it is hard to believe he gave the voluminous material contained in Urantia, without ever asking the ones conducting the readings what they were getting readings on. If he knew, it is hardly conceivable that he kept the information to himself and never mentioned it to his wife or family.

In spite of the case John has made for a connection between Edgar Cayce and *The Urantia Book* it seems to me there are equally strong arguments against such a connection.

E. E. Cayce 1998

———————— ∼ ————————

During the year following the first publication of this book, many times I thought about Edgar Evans Cayce's comments concerning the angelic names so prevalent in the Urantia Book which were not in the Cayce readings. If Cayce was indeed the source, how could it be explained that such very different material came through him? The clue to the answer to this mystery was found in the readings.

Halaliel, an angelic being who spoke through Cayce during a reading, volunteered to help make everything clearer for those listening, since the language used in the readings was difficult to follow. He needed the permission from the group to do so, but the offer of his help was declined. Some of the group thought that his help should have been accepted. So it was decided to take another reading and ask if the right decision had been made when Halaliel's help was refused. The answer was that the correct decision had been made and further it was stated that information should only be sought from the highest source, which is Christ or God. Any other source was certain to provide less than accurate information.

From the above example, I learned that it was possible for various spiritual entities to speak through Cayce while he was asleep.

Now I consider the Urantia Book and I can't help but notice that none of the material in the book originated with Christ or God. All of it came from other sources, ranging from the minds of mortals of the past and present, to various celestial personalities listed as authors in the table of contents.

If Cayce was the sleeping subject, this could be the reason for discrepancies between the Cayce readings and The Urantia Book. I discussed this idea with Edgar Evans Cayce on 12/30/99. His reply was, "It is certainly a possibility."

JB

———————— ∼ ————————

Comments by Meredith J. Sprunger

When John Bunker first told me that he was examining the possibility that Edgar Cayce was the contact person whose Thought Adjuster was used in transmitting the Urantia Papers, I assumed that it was an irrelevant exercise. After reading the completed manuscript presenting his findings, I was surprised both by the extent of his research and the possible relevance of some of his discoveries.

I, personally, regard my extended discussions with Dr. Sadler about the origin of the Urantia Papers as the most reliable information on the subject.

It would not bother me if Edgar Cayce or any other individual was the contact person. The evaluation of *The Urantia Book*, in my opinion, must be determined by the spiritual quality of the papers themselves. Research and speculation regarding the identity of the contact person is certainly a legitimate and interesting activity for those who are so motivated. I should like to congratulate John for his extensive and interesting research. *Edgar Cayce and The Urantia Book* is also a valuable treatise for bringing together historical information associated with the origin of *The Urantia Book*.

Even though this book presents interesting and possibly relevant information about Edgar Cayce and the Urantia Papers, I think the question concerning the contact person associated with the Urantia Papers is still open.

Meredith
1998

Comments by Martin Gardner
Author of *Urantia: The Great Cult Mystery*

Dear John:

I spent all day yesterday zipping through your book. Again, thank you <u>very</u> much for the typescript, and for the book's several references to my book.

First, let me say you write extremely well! And the amount of research you did is truly awesome. I learned a lot I didn't before know, especially about Cayce.

I think the strongest arguments for your theory that Cayce was the Urantia sleeper are the similarities you cite between Cayce readings and the UB. I was astonished by Cayce's assertion that Jesus and the angel Michael are the same! As you probably know, this unusual opinion is held by all Seventh-day Adventists and also by Urantians.

The strongest support for the claim that the sleeper was Wilfred is the chapter by Sherman in which he reports on what Sadler told him. Sadler said that when he lived in La Grange, the wife of a man in the same building came to him in distress, saying her husband was talking in his sleep and behaving strangely. Now the city directory of La Grange lists all the residents of the building where Sadler and his wife then lived. The only male resident who could possibly be the sleeper was Wilfred, living there with his wife shortly after his marriage.

As you know, Wilfred and his wife were, like Sadler, former devout Adventists. To me this explains how many SDA doctrines crept into the UB – soul sleeping until the body is reconstituted on another planet, the total annihilation of the wicked, the role of guardian angels, the famous misplaced comma in what Jesus said to the good thief on a cross beside him, the identity of Jesus and Michael, the plurality of inhabited planets, and the soon return of Jesus.

I was surprised to learn from you that Marcia's sister took all of Loose's letters. I wonder why. Loose was a bad influence on Sadler. He was a man of monstrous ego, capable of telling whopping lies to Sherman. His ego was almost as great as Sadler's. He constantly hinted he had something to do with the UB channeling, which he did not. He had not the slightest inkling of who the sleeper was.

You and I will have to have a friendly disagreement over the identity of the sleeper. No smoking gun is likely to turn up unless some old-timer who knows the truth will feel impelled to break the secrecy. Meanwhile, I greatly admire the work you've done on the mystery. As H.L. Mencken liked to write to correspondents, "you may be right."

All best,
Martin
12-25-2008

Karen's Introduction

When I met John in 1993, I was an avid *Urantia Book* reader with a basic knowledge of who Edgar Cayce was. I was not driven to locate the contact person for the book. After nearly twenty years of studying its content, I felt that it was so transforming that its origin was irrelevant to me. However, from almost the moment of our meeting, John and I were constantly falling upon information that seemed to tie *The Urantia Book* and Edgar Cayce together. It compelled us to give attention to the possibility that there was a real connection between them.

After five years of some astounding discoveries, we have decided that it is time to make our findings available. Although they are not necessarily conclusive, some will find that the evidence is overwhelming that Edgar Cayce was involved in a very important way with the inception of *The Urantia Book*. For others, there will be many questions and holes in the argument for that theory. Either way, I think this work is a valuable collection of well-documented and thoroughly researched facts worthy of consideration by any student of either the Urantia concepts or the Cayce material. The big reward for anyone who takes a look is that these two happenings in our history, whether directly related or not, bear so much life-changing and eye-opening information for the development of our souls and our planet that we would do well to give them both serious consideration in our search for truth. This book has more to offer than the presentation of an opinion. It is a wealth of little known information, and if it doesn't change anyone's opinion about *The Urantia Book* or the Cayce readings, it still stands as a valuable resource for students.

Various discoveries really made me think twice about my skepticism that Cayce may, indeed, have been at the center of the activities bringing about *The Urantia Book*. For example, we located a book written in 1959 about Sir Hubert Wilkins, a famous Arctic explorer who had a side interest in psychic phenomena and was a participant in the Urantia revelation. In this biography, previously unknown to the Urantia organizations, a letter is reprinted from Wilkins to his secretary in which he says that the contact person for *The Urantia Book* was, up to that day, unaware of his participation in the project. That gave an explanation for the gnawing question as to how Cayce could have been involved with no evidence of it left behind.

Another very interesting fact was noted in Dr. William Sadler's book, *The Mind at Mischief*. Sadler lived in Chicago where Cayce was making headline news at the time *The Urantia Book* was being drafted. An anonymous case discussed as 'exceptional' in the appendix of his book is now known to have been the contact person for *The Urantia Book*. It is interesting that Cayce so closely matches the unique phenomenon of the person described in that appendix. Both were considered to be 'in a class by themselves'.

The book you are now holding gives many such thought-provoking facts. It includes timelines for both the Cayce and Urantia incidents that have some truly uncanny parallels. It lays out a scenario, based on well-documented evidence, which proves opportunity existed for the collaboration between Sadler and Cayce. It gives a reasonable explanation for the secrecy that kept even the contact person himself unaware of his involvement. It provides plausible explanations for the obvious differences in both the language and content of the resulting documents from the two happenings. It is a labor of love, in hopes of unclouding truth. It is a springboard from which thinking individuals can go forward with an expanded perspective. It proposes a hypothesis that will, no doubt, inspire debate among people who have found comfort and strength in both schools of thought. In the spirit of peace, harmony and love among all the people of the earth, it is my hope that we have found one more way to bring the various elements of truth together toward a clearer *wholeness* of truth.

Karen L. Pressler

John's Introduction to the First Edition

I shared the information contained in this manuscript with my friend David Kruse, who is an attorney. After reviewing it, he commented that he believed he could convince a jury, if it were a civil case, that Edgar Cayce was the sleeping subject.

Personally, I believe that Edgar Cayce was the person used for the transmission of some of the information contained within *The Urantia Book*. Portions of the book obviously came from other sources, as you shall see. But in the final analysis you must decide for yourself.

During the past twenty-four years, I have studied *The Urantia Book*. During the past five years, I have compared it to the Cayce readings, and read every book I could find about Cayce. I have observed that a great amount of information has been withheld and/or destroyed concerning the origin of *The Urantia Book*. I have experienced a substantial amount of ridicule because of my investigation. But I have learned: "Any theory, hypothesis, philosophy, sect, creed, or institution, that fears investigation, openly manifests its own error."[1]

Nevertheless, I have found the experience of being subjected to both sources of information to have been a mind expanding one. Both sources helped me grow and led me into a deeper understanding of myself. My life has been forever changed for the better.

I am experiencing the power of Harmony, Peace, Love, and Understanding at work in my life, now, today! I have learned a greater respect for God and deeper love for my fellows! To me, these are the *most important* results of this research, because they help make the world a better place in which to live.

---

[1] Andrew Jackson Davis, *Nature's Divine Revelations A Voice to Mankind*, (New York, NY: Trow's Printing and Bookbinding Co., 1847; thirty-fourth edition, Boston, MA: Banner of Light Publishing House, 1886), p. 1

Six years ago, I found myself requiring collateral information to help support my belief system and I began searching for supporting evidence. I questioned who wrote *The Urantia Book*. The answer I encountered from other readers was that divine spiritual beings had been the source for it. A human being had also been involved, but he was merely a microphone through which they spoke. But who was he?

Mankind was not meant to know, I was informed. Allegedly, these spiritual beings did not want a human name attached to the book, because they wished not to create another saint for future generations to venerate. After giving that answer some thought, I reasoned that I did not worship Paul the Apostle, Matthew, Moses or any other person who was credited as authoring any other sacred writing in the Bible. I could not locate any statement in *The Urantia Book* that said the identity of the sleeping subject should be kept secret, therefore that answer dissatisfied me. What I did find in *The Urantia Book* was this: "Facts and truth court the full light of comprehension and rejoice in the illumination and enlightenment of scientific research."[2]

While in Chicago in 1994, Karen and I browsed around in a bookstore, one day prior to attending our very first *Urantia Book* Conference at Northwestern University, in Evanston, Illinois. A book titled *There is a River: The Story of Edgar Cayce*[3] caught my eye. I had heard Cayce's name only a very few times during my life. All I knew about him was that he talked in his sleep. A book of this type was nothing that would normally interest me. There were plenty of other books to choose from, but I was drawn back to that one. I don't know why I picked up Cayce's book. I really didn't know anything about him. I prefer books on science subjects, such as

---

[2] *The Urantia Book* (Chicago: Urantia Foundation, 1955) 991.
[3] Thomas Sugrue, *There is a River: The Story of Edgar Cayce* (Virginia Beach, Va.: A.R.E. Press, 1973).

archaeology or paleontology. In my hotel room that night I started reading the story of Edgar Cayce.

That is where all this began.

John M. Bunker

John's Introduction to the Second Edition

After reading the first edition of this book, both Meredith Sprunger and Edgar Evans Cayce exhibited the sentiment that there was a greater possibility that Cayce was involved in Urantia than either of them had realized before. Their comments that appeared in the first edition were made after they read one of the rough drafts and before they read the finished book. When the first edition was finally completed, it contained additional information that had not yet been discovered when the first draft was created. After reading the completed book, even though he still has some reservations Edgar Evans Cayce reservedly admitted, "it is certainly a possibility" that some of the information in *The Urantia Book* may have originated with Edgar Cayce. Meredith Sprunger remarked, "I had no idea that so many people were involved with both Cayce and *The Urantia Book*. I look forward to the second edition of your book."

I now know that at least three of Dr. Sadler's Forum members were associated with Cayce; Harold Sherman, Mrs. 3316, and Nola Smith. Nola is my latest discovery. She was the handwriting expert who was involved with Dr. Sadler. Her story of the event was different than the traditional story I have heard passed on by readers of *The Urantia Book*. One of her associates was Milton N. Bunker. There was also a Mr. Bunker mentioned in one of Cayce's readings.

In *The Mind at Mischief*, Dr. Sadler stated that the forces speaking through the sleeping subject were "always in a most positive manner" antagonistic toward communications with deceased mortals. This is precisely the attitude of the forces that spoke through the sleeping Cayce.

Another discovery seems noteworthy, since there is a story in circulation among the long time readers of *The Urantia Book* that the revelators who spoke through the sleeping subject had made previous attempts to communicate with our world.

About one hundred years before the events occurred with Dr. Sadler and his sleeping subject, another doctor had a sleeping subject and published a book that came through verbally while the man was unconscious. The book is titled *The Principles of Nature, Her Divine Revelations, and a Voice to Mankind.* The doctor had a stenographer take down everything the man said. The doctor claimed that except for grammar and punctuation, he made no changes in the text. The book claims flatly to be a revelation. In Appendix F I have listed some of the words and ideas that appear synonymous with Cayce's readings and *The Urantia Book.*

And last, but perhaps not least, I have discovered evidence that Cayce was responsible for Harold Sherman going to work for Warner Brothers and becoming reacquainted with Harry Loose and thereby meeting Dr. Sadler and becoming involved in the Urantia project!

Our investigation continues. This second edition includes additional material that was discovered during the past three years that have elapsed since the first printing was released in April 1999.

John M. Bunker
1/24/2003

Preface

Dr. William Sadler was an investigator of the paranormal and had an unusual interest in spiritualistic phenomenon. At one time he worked with Howard Thurston, the famous magician, in the exposure of fake and fraudulent mediums.[4] He investigated and debunked many psychics and clairvoyants in his pursuit of knowledge of spirituality and his attempt to understand the subconscious mind. In his book *The Mind at Mischief*, he gives 1909 as the year he established the Chicago Institute of Research and Diagnosis, where he spent upwards of twenty years investigating and studying a large number of clairvoyants, psychics, and mediums.[5] At that time in history, medical science tended to kill as many patients as it managed to cure.[6] Therefore the public turned to psychics and mediums as an alternative source for healing and medical advice. Unscrupulous mediums cheated the public out of millions of dollars, money for which the medical profession competed. The AMA and its members waged a war against psychics and mediums. These circumstances helped fuel Sadler's efforts to debunk fraudulent psychics and enlighten the public.

Conversely, the information Cayce gave in his readings was saving lives and healing the sick. He was receiving nation-wide attention as a result of Dr. Wesley Ketchum telling the story of his dealings with Cayce at a meeting of the National Society of Homeopathic Physicians during a visit to California. Ketchum also prepared a paper about Cayce that was submitted and read to the American Society of Clinical Research in Boston in September of 1910. (Incidentally, the president of this Society was from Chicago, where Sadler lived.) As a result of Ketchum's paper, this headline appeared in the New York *Times* on

---

[4] Meussling, 42.
[5] Sadler, preface, *Mind at Mischief*, vii.
[6] Meussling, 4.

October 9, 1910: "Illiterate man becomes doctor when hypnotized." Thereafter, many newspapers across the country printed similar stories:

-Seattle *Times* 10/15/10
        "Psychic Power New to Medical World"
-New York *Times* 10/15/10
        "Psychic Power New to Medical World"
-Cincinnati *Times-Star* 10/10/10
        "Man's Strange Power Puzzling Physicians"
-Kansas City *Post*
        "Youth in Trance Diagnoses Disease"
-The Oregon *Sunday Journal*
        "Kentucky Farmer Effects Cures While in Trance"
-Chicago *Examiner* 10/15/10
        "Possessed Psychic Powers"
-Chicago *Examiner* 10/15/10
        "Can See Disease While in Trance"

As time passed and my research continued, I became more convinced that Edgar Cayce was connected with *The Urantia Book*. I wondered if the reason that the text of *The Urantia Book* differed so much from the Cayce readings might have been due to the editorship of Dr. William Sadler, although Dr. Sadler claimed he did not edit the material. I also considered that Dr. Sadler may have gathered information from more than one psychic individual, since he studied so many of them. However, even if he did, I could not ignore the resemblance of *The Urantia Book* to some of the Cayce material.

During the first five years of this investigation, I have found many similarities from the Cayce readings contained in *The Urantia Book*. Many of them are exact matches while some are identical ideas worded differently.

There are also some glaring differences, such as the absence in the Cayce readings of the angelic hierarchy, described in such detail in *The Urantia Book*. But Cayce did occasionally give messages from angelic beings, whom he mentioned by name.

Perhaps this can be viewed as a similarity, rather than a difference.

Another difference is The Urantia Book's stand against the idea of reincarnation, which is so prevalent in the Cayce material. But it is also true that in the days of Jesus, reincarnation and resurrection meant the same thing.

The differences in the text of The Urantia Book and the Cayce material are plain to see. It is the similarities that require insight. However, it was not only the text, but many minute details in the lives of the people involved, the timing, and the events that converged together to indicate that Cayce was the solitary suspect for being Dr. Sadler's anonymous sleeping subject. These are abundant to the smallest detail.

For whatever reasons, Dr. Sadler did not believe in full disclosure of all the facts. His attempts to reveal less than complete detailed information about the origin of the Urantia Papers have resulted in this mystery.

Part I: Overview and Historical Facts

Edgar Cayce -- The Sleeping Subject

1. Introduction

Because *The Urantia Book* is a relatively unknown publication among the general public, Edgar Evans Cayce suggested that I explain what it is and the fact that its source is unknown. Edgar Evans Cayce is the youngest son of the psychic healer, Edgar Cayce. This book is my effort to clear up the mysteries behind the reception of the Urantia Papers, which resulted in a 2097 page volume discussing the nature of God, his hierarchy of universe assistants, world pre-history, the history of the universe, evolution, and the life of Jesus.

The Urantia Book attempts to integrate science, religion, and philosophy. Similarly, the Cayce readings achieve a synthesis between science, religion, and philosophy.[7] I believe this is a similarity that is more substantial than it first appears to be. I believe Edgar Cayce was the unknown contact person for *The Urantia Book*, and in this book I will present the results of five and one half years of research, which have brought me to that conclusion.

It began as a quest to find the truth about the authorship of *The Urantia Book*. If you are familiar with *The Urantia Book* you will find this information very thought provoking. If you are more familiar with the Edgar Cayce readings, you will find this story of interest because it illustrates Cayce's involvement in a project of which he had no conscious knowledge.

The Association for Research and Enlightenment (A.R.E.) was formed around Cayce's work, and contains records of all of the documentation connected with the readings he gave and his correspondence. There is only one mention of the word Urantia in their files. Someone from the Urantia Brotherhood[8]

---

[7] Gina Cerminara, *Many Mansions* (New York: Morrow, 1967) 45.

[8] See Dr. Sadler's papers (Appendix A of this book), "The Urantia Brotherhood", 192210, for more information about this group.

mailed a copy of the book to the A.R.E. in 1955. She is identified as Mrs. 3316[9] and was a Forum member[10] who spent twenty years studying the Urantia Papers before they were published. She also received readings from Cayce and made trips to the A.R.E. in Virginia Beach. Because of privacy, the A.R.E. will not reveal her name. The first record of the A.R.E. receiving a letter from her was in 1943. The following is an unedited letter she wrote on November 11, 1955 to Hugh Lynn Cayce, Edgar's first son:

> After some thot I have decided to send a new book, in which I am interested, to the research library there at Virginia Beach. It is the history and story of this planet from its beginning. In this instance our planet is called or named "Urantia", the book is named *The Urantia Book.*" The history includes geologic, geographic, civilization -- religious, -- any and all things pertaining to this planet. Discussion groups have had access to these manuscripts and papers for 25 years. I, myself have read them for over 20 years and was very glad when a Foundation was formed to compile and publish them in book form. Authors are messengers and certain personalities interested in reaching the human family and earth to widen our concept of the Universe and many Universes of Time & Space. My interest in the above in no way interfered with my interest in the Cayce papers or readings. *In fact, I think they infuse together, in a way,* at least it has been so with me. The god-plan for us all is so very vast -- and the mental development so different with so, so many of us -- I feel that information is being released thru many sources to meet the spiritual hunger of today.

---

[9] Readings are considered confidential and are referred to by numbers rather than names.

[10] See Dr. Sadler's papers (Appendix A of this book),"How the Forum Started", 181198, for more information about this group.

Any books of Truth can be used beneficially for a group -- analysis which will disturb complacency of conviction indicates growth -- yet always the question still confronts us -- what kinds of basic contradictions concerning man and history and God give the most secure foundations for social reforms, the quest for justice, and the advice for man's freedom? Enclosed is a card that I would suggest that [be attached] to the fly leaf in some manner. I am sending out several of these books and sending yours as it came from the publishers -- it was so well packed, I did not open it to insert card. *These papers came through in much the same way as Mr. Cayce's readings* and may well become the most controversial collection in book form as any book of the next 25 to 30 years. It is being launched quietly and unobtrusively so as to meet many thotful minds before a fury could make it die aborning, or at least retard its forward movement. It is not a new religion nor a new church. No one needs to read, believe it or even know about it "to be saved." It merely widens the knowledge of what we already know -- stressing the Brotherhood of Man and the Fatherhood of God. I can assure you many people of prominence have read and greatly appreciated the information in this book. Books can be purchased (for the present) thru the "Urantia Brotherhood" 533 Diversey Parkway, Chicago -- a non-profit organization, not a salaried job in the "office" as of now -- all for the cause! Please excuse this not to well written letter -- my arthritis affects my hands and eyes today but I did not want to delay this project of mine any longer. (I'm ambulatory and fairly comfortable -- just have off days -- so I'm quite alright.) Mr. Cayce gave me a reading in '43 -- I understand my "case" pretty well thru him -- I have been to Virginia Beach -- enjoyed it all very much -- especially the conference of about five years ago when I was visiting a daughter in Norfolk. Have been an Associate Member of A.R.E. two different times for years, but shall have to give up my membership for the present as my promise to myself to send out a few *Urantia Books* has taken over the budget and I must cut several corners for a time at least. I shall miss hearing from you, I think the work you are all doing is most important and timely -- you are reaching out and helping so many.[11] [emphasis mine]

On June 3, 1944 another individual, Miss 3681 (A.R.E. reference number) wrote to Edgar Cayce, "Have you read *The Mind at Mischief*? I have forgotten the author's name, but what he wrote in the last chapter interested me greatly and I wondered if he were referring to your wonderful works."[12]

Cayce did not answer this question, but the author to whom Miss 3681 was referring, Dr. William Sadler, was in fact writing about the Urantia contact person.

Another Forum member and member of The Seventy, who was also a member of Cayce's organization The Association for Research and Enlightenment, was Nola Smith.

Nola Smith

Nola moved to Chicago in the mid 1930's. While living there, she purchased a book titled The Mind at Mischief. She was very impressed with the contents of that book and noticed that the author, Dr. William S. Sadler, resided in Chicago. She discovered Dr. Sadler's telephone number in the Chicago telephone directory and called him. She told him that she had read his book and that she wanted to meet him. He set an appointment to meet with her the following week. She found

---

[11] *The Complete Edgar Cayce Readings*, CD-ROM (Virginia Beach, VA: A.R.E. Press, 1993) Document #42980, 3316-001 Reports, contains a portion of the letter. The complete letter is available in the A.R.E. archives.

[12] *The Complete Edgar Cayce Readings*, Document #44740, 3681-001 (2/18/44).

the doctor to be a friendly, fatherly type gentleman. After their initial visit, he asked her to come back the following week for another visit. From week to week, their visits continued and he eventually told her about the Urantia papers. Nola joined the Forum and spent time each day reading the papers at 533 Diversey Parkway. She met Lena Sadler, Bill Jr., and other Forum members who included Sir Wilkins, Sir Hillary, and Harold & Martha Sherman.

Nola was one of the founders of The Chicago School of Grapho Analysis, a school that taught its students to recognize personality traits exhibited in an individual's handwriting by the style or form of the writing. Dr. Sadler asked for an analysis of his and Bill, Jr.'s handwriting. Nola analyzed Bill, Jr.'s handwriting, while John analyzed Dr. Sadler's handwriting.

Thereafter, Dr. Sadler sent Lena and Bill Jr. to visit Nola's school, because he thought that this type of information might be helpful to both of them in their professions.

Nola's colleagues were Milton Bunker and John Silvi. Milton was a recognized expert in the field of handwriting analysis and he was also an author of several books on the subject. John Silvi worked at the school with Nola, but Milton acted more as a consultant to John and Nola, than as a teacher at the school. Nola co-authored a book on handwriting analysis with John Silvi titled *What and Why*, which was published with assistance from Milton. Nola introduced John to the Urantia information, but Milton was not interested in it.

During the early 1940's, Nola worked for Bill Sadler, Jr. at his consulting business, while she also worked at the school. This came about because Bill's firm screened candidates for executive positions for several Chicago firms. Bill administered a battery of tests to each candidate. One of the tests he used was handwriting analysis, which was handled by Nola. Nola's job was to recognize unwanted personality traits through the handwriting of the person taking the test.

During these years Nola became very closely acquainted with the Sadlers. She spent time every day reading the Urantia papers, was a regular member of the Forum, and became a member of the Seventy. She left Chicago in 1955 to move to Arizona with her mother, because the climate was considered to be advantageous for her mother's ailing health.

On several occasions during the early 1940's, Dr. Sadler brought handwriting samples from his patients to Nola. Nola never knew the identity of the patients. She was asked by the doctor to analyze personality characteristics that were recognizable from the handwriting. This is the origin of the story that refers to Dr. Sadler calling in handwriting experts to analyze the handwriting of the sleeping subject. [13] Nola said that to the best of her knowledge, there were no other handwriting experts involved with Dr. Sadler. When asked if she ever made any determination as to whether any of the handwriting was written by the same person or not, she said, "No."

Nola was surprised to hear the story that originated with Dr. Sadler in 1956, when he met with a group of ministers from Indiana. One of the members of that group of ministers was Dr. Meredith J. Sprunger. Meredith and Irene Sprunger both stated that Dr. Sadler revealed to them that handwriting experts were called in on the phenomenon of the sleeping subject. Further, these handwriting experts determined that the handwriting used to write down the Urantia papers was not that of the sleeping subject. Mark Kulieke revealed the same information in his book Birth of a Revelation.

Since Nola was the only handwriting expert affiliated with Dr. Sadler, she concludes that either Meredith, Irene, and Mark are all mistaken, or Dr. Sadler must have meant that the handwriting was that of the stenographer who took notes while the sleeping subject spoke. Nola said Dr. Sadler was a very smart man and he would not make this kind of a mistake.

---

[13] Telephone conversation, 6/6/99 between the author and Nola Smith.

The Urantia Book was published in 1955 by the Urantia Foundation and the 'human author' of the book was never revealed. The Foundation named itself as author when applying for the original copyright. Upon petition for renewal of copyright many years later, the Foundation named the author as being William Sadler, Jr. When a third party challenged the copyright, the Foundation alleged that William Sadler, Jr. wrote only the 'Table of Contents' and they did not know the identity of the 'human author.'

There are no original records and practically no material available concerning the beginning of the development of *The Urantia Book*. The group of people who formed the Urantia Foundation intentionally destroyed nearly all of these materials.

In 1995, after one year of comparing the Cayce material with the Urantia material, it was my belief that *The Urantia Book* was a composite of material that was based upon information obtained through Edgar Cayce while he was in an unconscious state. Further, I believed that Mr. Cayce was never told that he was used for this purpose. At that point in my investigation, I could not explain how such a thing could have been perpetuated for so many years. I knew from studying Cayce that unless he was told about the readings after he awoke, he never remembered a thing. Thus, I reasoned that if he was the sleeping subject, he never knew it.

After reaching this conclusion, I traveled to Virginia Beach to discuss my thinking with Edgar Cayce's son, Edgar Evans Cayce. At that time I had no supporting evidence for my hypothesis, just intuition and deductive reasoning. Edgar Evans Cayce asked me to explain how, if his father gave readings for the Urantia material, neither he nor anyone else in the family had ever heard anything about it?

It wasn't until later that I discovered evidence and a witness to support my theory, which will be explained later in this story. This is often how the process went: when I learned what questions to ask, the answers presented themselves!

The investigation that I conducted began in April 1994. I have accumulated many pieces of information since then, and will be telling you the story of how I believe the people and events fit together which led to the publication of *The Urantia Book*.

2. The Significance of Language

The language of the Cayce readings is nothing like that of *The Urantia Book*. Perhaps this can be explained, in part, by understanding that readings, when given to specialists in their field, were given in terminology appropriate to that level of understanding. Conversely, readings spoken to average persons of that day and time (many of whom experienced more religious teaching than secular education) often contained the use of 'thee' and 'thou', or basic everyday terms.

But when speaking to physicians, the readings were amazing in their delivery.[14] Here is what Dr. Wesley Ketchum reported to the American Society of Clinical research in Boston, which also appeared in a New York *Times* article on 10/9/10:

> His [Cayce's] language is usually of the best, and his psy-chologic terms and description of the nervous anatomy would do credit to any professor of nervous anatomy, and there is no faltering in his speech and all his statements are clear and concise. He handles the most complex 'jaw breakers' with as much ease as any Boston physician, which to me is quite wonderful, in view of the fact that while in his normal state he is an illiterate man, especially along the line of medicine, surgery, or pharmacy, of which he knows nothing.[15]

Harmon Hartzell Bro, Ph.D., who witnessed over 500 of Cayce's readings, said:

> Cayce himself was uneducated beyond grade school. Yet twice a day for years he had entered, through prayer, a puzzling semi-hypnotic state of altered consciousness, where he was able to speak with quiet accuracy the technical language

---

[14] Harmon H. Bro, *Edgar Cayce on Religion and Psychic Experience* (New York: Harper & Row, 1971) 28.
[15] *The Complete Edgar Cayce Readings*, Document #7840, 0294-001 Reports, (10/9/10).

of medicine and pharmacy, the precise terminology and even
the trade jargon of stockbrokers and engineers and deep-sea
divers, the central philosophic terms of traditions Eastern and
Western, and the alien names of individuals and places and
groups and customs from cultures stretching backward from
the present to the dawn of history. More than once he had
shown to competent observers that he could offer counsel in
foreign languages which he had never learned.[16]

Latin was sometimes used within the readings although
Cayce himself had no knowledge of foreign languages. One
example is the Latin word 'minutia', pronounced 'my-new-
sha'. This word illustrates how use of the 'tia' combination
gives a 'sha' sound. It may also suggest that the word Urantia
is actually derived from Latin, or some other closely related
branch of the Italic languages. The Cayce readings include
words from Latin and other extinct languages.

The word *urania* is of Latin origin and refers to astronomy
and also heavens. One of Dr. Sadler's associates, Sir Hubert
Wilkins, explained that the meaning of the word Urantia was
'our universe.'[17] *The Urantia Book* refers to itself as "the narrative of your local universe." [18]

In Latin, "t" is the nineteenth letter of the alphabet and is
interchanged with "s" and assimilated with "s". The "t" also
has another function in Latin: it can be used to represent a praenomen, which means 'first name.' The word 'praenomen' is
actually a compound word consisting of two root words:

Prae which means first or in front of or before.
Nomen which means name.

---

[16] Harmon H. Bro, *Begin a New Life* (New York: Harper & Row, 1971) 8.
[17] John Grierson, *Sir Hubert Wilkins: The Enigma of Exploration* (London: Robert Hale, [1959?]) 202.
[18] *The Urantia Book*, 337.

When the use of "**t**" is incorporated to modify the word urania, the word changes from meaning sky or heavens to meaning *the first name* of our sky or heavens, and can be used interchangeably to mean our universe, or our world. The English language is not an original language, but rather a composite of words and ideas taken from other more ancient languages.

An illustration of this comes from the English usage of the Latin word "prae." It is changed to "pre" and the definition is modified, but retains a similar meaning as the Latin from which it is derived: 'earlier than' or 'prior to', as in *prehistoric*. Consider the word *urania* + t = urantia:

uran = sky or heaven[19]
ia = Latin suffix denoting abstracts[20]
urania = astronomy (broader perspective of sky or
    heaven)[21]
t = shows first, earlier and/or <prehistoric> name
urantia = our universe, our sky, our heaven (our
    place in the universe)

I suspect that some of the unusual words in *The Urantia Book* are derivatives from Latin. Reading 1745-1 contains the phrase, "Dum Tacent Clamant!"[22] The translation of this phrase is, "While they are silent, they cry aloud." Upon checking the definition of these words, I discovered that Modern Latin uses the word 'Tum', but not 'Dum'.

Further investigation revealed that Latin is merely one of the dialects spoken by the Latini, a group of related tribes who settled in the territory of Latium (la-sha-um). Certain changes of sounds, forms, syntax, and meaning arose over time within these Italic dialects. For example, in one of the ancient Italic

---

[19] *Oxford Latin Dictionary* (Oxford University Press, 1983).
[20] *Oxford Latin Dictionary.*
[21] *Oxford Latin Dictionary.*
[22] *The Complete Edgar Cayce Readings*, Document #41434, 3042-001 Text (5/31/43).

dialects, the letter 't' becomes 'd'. The Latin language used in the readings dates back to the time of antiquity.[23]

In The *Urantia Book*, 87 unique words with an 'ia' ending are used a total of 2,290 times. In the Cayce readings there are 481 different words with the 'ia' suffix used a total of 46,805 times. In Latin, 'ia' is a suffix that means: "Things from, relating to, as in: personalia." Perhaps Latin is the source language for *The Urantia Book* and the Cayce material.

According to Dr. Harmon Bro, there were also instances of Cayce giving readings in German[24] and Italian, while some words or names used in the readings were actually from forgotten, extinct, prehistoric languages, like Mayan, Persian and Ancient Egyptian.[25]

Dr. Gina Cerminara, Ph.D., who lived with the Cayce family for two years, was a very perceptive observer and articulate scholar. Her observations reveal another similarity to the Urantia phenomenon. (i.e., the unknown language mechanism which was utilized during the transmission of the text of the Urantia papers)

She gives insights into the language of the Cayce readings in the following excerpts from an article she wrote for the A.R.E. Bulletin, and sheds some light on the difficulties in the transmission of higher-dimensional concepts:

> Exactly what the language mechanism was has never been explained by the readings themselves, except for very fragmentary remarks to the effect that higher-dimensional realities cannot easily be expressed in three-dimensional terms. This sounds reasonable. And piecing together what the readings themselves have said with the linguistic

---

[23] L.R. Palmer, *The Latin Language* (London: Faber & Faber, Ltd., 1954) Chap. 1.

[24] Doris Agee, *Edgar Cayce on ESP* (New York: Warner Books, 1983) 65.

[25] *The Complete Edgar Cayce Readings*, (various readings over a twenty year period).

impressions one gathers on examining the readings, one arrives at some fairly satisfactory conclusions.

1. the readings sound like a man speaking in a foreign language;
2. they sound like a person from an ancient era trying to speak to a modern era;
3. they sound like a highly educated person – or an academician – trying to make himself clear to the uneducated – or the non-academic.

The first impression – that of a man trying to speak in a foreign language – is very strong. The English language is notoriously difficult for foreigners.

The stiltedness of many passages in the readings give rise to still another impression – that of an individual educated far above the level of the person to whom he is talking, and attempting to talk down to the level of the second person.

This offers both psychological and linguistic difficulties. This may be due to that kind of social ineptitude that arises from many years of academic seclusion. There is among this type of persons a genuine habituation to certain language constructions, which they can depart from only with great effort. The breadth, subtlety, and complexity of their thought is something to which the uneducated are not accustomed. The necessity, then, to make themselves intelligible to people whose outlook is innocent of ideological or technical preoccupations, and whose speech is rough and ready for the simple purposes of making a living, is often a difficult one.

The difficulty of self-expression, which was obviously experienced by the giver of information in the readings, seems quite comparable.

It must be remembered that the readings were given from a point of view of an enlarged consciousness – the source of information was conversant with many dimensions, and needed to condense what he knew into

*3-dimensionsal terms. This is a difficult thing for us
to grasp, because we are so completely imbedded in a
3-dimensional consciousness that we can not conceive
of realities of 4,5,6,7, and more dimensions. The
difficulty involved is in compressing knowledge into
narrower terms than those really adequate to describe
it.[26]*

The grammar used in the Cayce material is sometimes difficult to follow because no effort was ever made to revise or
modify it. The readings were simply copied down verbatim so
that their meaning would not be changed.

In the case of *The Urantia Book*, modification of the original
text took place over a period of many years, some information
was added, some deleted.[27] Much information and many
hundreds of pages of written material existed before the official
start of the revelatory process in 1924. While the information
was somewhat more general, it formed a basis for the Urantia
Papers to a certain extent. Some of the same facts and truths
that are in the book were in this earlier material,[28] which was
destroyed from time to time when it was no longer needed, *or
for other reasons*. Additional material was shredded upon the
death of Dr. Sadler, and his daughter Christy authorized the
destruction of the last portions during her final illness.[29]

---

[26] *The Complete Edgar Cayce Readings*, Document #4028, 0254-063 Reports,
    reference to A.R.E Bulletin (dated 12/45) article by Dr. Gina Cerminara,
    Ph.D., "The Language of the Cayce Readings."
[27] Dr. Sadler's papers (see Appendix A of this book) 184202.
    Mark Kulieke, *Birth of a Revelation* (Green Bay, Wis.: Morning Star
    Foundation, 1994) 3.
[28] Kulieke, 3.
[29] Kulieke, 6.

Edgar Evans Cayce & Hugh Lynn Cayce

3. Missing Cayce Readings

Edgar Evans Cayce informs me that copies of many of the readings given from the early 1900's to the early 1920's are not on file at the Association for Research and Enlightenment. The A.R.E. was established by Cayce to preserve the readings. There are over 14,000 readings on file and although the collection is substantial, it is incomplete. Hugh Lynn Cayce concurs that the files assembled through the years are far from complete.[30] Dr. Harmon Bro revealed that records of everything Cayce did were not kept until after the halfway point in his career.[31]

Edgar Cayce's secretary, Gladys Davis Turner stated, "we will possibly never know exactly how many readings Edgar Cayce gave, since a record of so many of them was not kept."[32]

In 1933, Cayce said, "It would not be an exaggeration to say that I have been in the unconscious state (during which the readings are given) perhaps twenty-five thousand times during the last thirty-one years."[33]

For the next eleven years after making this statement, Cayce usually gave two or more readings each day, until his final illness in late 1944, which would have amounted to about 8,000 readings.

During the last years of his life, Cayce sometimes pushed himself to give more than two readings per day, although that was all the readings themselves recommended. Sometimes he gave four, six, eight and more per day.[34] Some days he spent 3

---

[30] Hugh Lynn Cayce, *Venture Inward* (New York: Harper & Row, 1964) 28.

[31] Bro, *Edgar Cayce on Religion and Psychic Experience*, 18.

[32] *The Complete Edgar Cayce Readings*, Document #57192, 5780-001 Reports (1/1/23).

[33] Agee, 23.

[34] Bro, *Edgar Cayce on Religion & Psychic Experience*, 30.
   Lytle W. Robinson, *Is it True What They Say About Edgar Cayce?* (New York: Berkley Books, 1979) 178.

or 4 hours unconscious, instead of the familiar total of an hour to an hour and a half.[35]

The above referenced information indicates that Cayce could have given 33,000 (or more!) readings during his lifetime. But the A.R.E. contains transcripts of only slightly over 14,000 readings. This allows for the possibility that the Urantia material could have been channeled during some of the thousands of missing readings.

---

[35] Bro, *Edgar Cayce on Religion & Psychic Experience*, 247.

20

4. The Effects of Secrecy

Edgar Evans Cayce told me that he had never heard people mention any readings remotely comparable to the Urantia material. This may be reasonably explained, considering that there was an enormous effort exerted to maintain secrecy by those people who published *The Urantia Book*. This group was known as the Forum and all members were required to sign pledges of secrecy. All original transcripts of messages were burned as soon as they were typed. It may be that this secrecy was motivated by the following contingencies.

Professional Ethics and Confidentiality

By maintaining the confidentiality of the psychics and mediums which he investigated, including the identity of the 'sleeping subject', Dr. Sadler was practicing the code of professional ethics governing his profession. He never to secured permission for the complete reporting of the phenomenon connected with the unusual case of the sleeping subject.[36]

The Threat of the American Medical Association

In the early 1900's, the American Medical Association had taken a staunch position against psychics and mediums. The famous magicians Howard Thurston and Harry Houdini were representing themselves as psychic investigators and exposing fraudulent mediums. Dr. Sadler was also participating in these efforts to debunk phony spiritualists. This was the scene of events when Cayce *again* traveled to Chicago, in July of 1924.

The readings had advised that Chicago was one possibility for establishing a hospital in which the treatments given in the

---

[36] William S. Sadler, *The Mind at Mischief* (New York and London: Funk & Wagnall's, 1929) 382.

readings could be administered correctly, under professional medical supervision.

Several business owners in Chicago, doctors (including a City Health Official) and the Mayor observed Cayce giving readings while he was in Chicago. They were all in favor of helping him establish a research center in the area.

During the course of these events, the readings warned that a situation was to arise which had not been taken into consideration: now was not the time to establish the Chicago facility. But everyone, *including Cayce*, ignored this warning, and continued to plan for the Chicago location of the proposed hospital.

Dr. Frisch was a wealthy, influential physician in Chicago, and he assured Cayce that he would make sure that there was no trouble for him from the authorities.

Dr. Frisch and a number of other Chicago doctors had been using Cayce's readings to diagnose and prescribe treatment for their patients.

Apparently, Dr. Frisch believed that by using an example of Cayce's medical diagnoses and prescribed treatment as evidence, he could convince the AMA of the merit of sanctioning the Cayce hospital as a research facility. Perhaps he reasoned that they would be convinced when presented with the results obtained from the readings. He even had a location in mind for the Cayce hospital and intended to make an offer to secure it.

However, Dr. Frisch's promise to take care of the authorities in Chicago backfired. When the AMA learned of the proposed research facility, they issued a bulletin to their members threatening the expulsion of any doctor who used Cayce's readings to prescribe treatment for patients. During the months that followed, doctors in Chicago were forced to abandon their association with Cayce or face the consequence of expulsion from the AMA and face public disgrace. Some doctors chose to maintain hidden contact with Cayce.

In the wake of these events, in September of 1925, a pledge of secrecy was required of the Forum members. This secrecy commenced 19 years after Dr. Sadler had first encountered the sleeping subject in 1906.

Since the publication of *The Urantia Book*, many readers have believed that the secrecy in the Forum began because of a request by the forces speaking through the sleeping subject. The general belief has been that those forces decided to operate under a veil of secrecy to protect the Urantia revelation, which by that time had begun. This may have been an incorrect assumption, because the first paper may not have yet appeared at the time the secrecy began.

From what source do I arrive at this speculation? In Dr. Sadler's *History of the Urantia Movement*, in the section titled "How the Urantia Papers Started," it is stated that sessions with the sleeping subject had been ongoing for about 20 years when a challenge came to ask more meaningful questions. Dr. Sadler shared this challenge with the Forum and they came up with hundreds of questions to ask to the sleeping subject about God and the universe. In response to these questions, the first Urantia Paper was produced.

The sleeping Cayce posed such a challenge in Mid-March of 1927. This was approximately 20 and 1/3 years after the autumn of 1906. If Cayce was Sadler's sleeping subject, it seems to me that secrecy in the Forum corresponded more with the threat of the AMA than with the timing of the first Urantia Paper. [37]

The foregoing reasons may have motivated the intense degree of secrecy concerning the Urantia material, and may explain why no one in Cayce's family ever heard of the Urantia readings. But Edgar Evans Cayce insisted that if his father had been involved with Urantia, he would not have withheld that fact from his family.

How can this be explained? Perhaps a clue to the answer is in the appendix of Dr. William Sadler's book, *The Mind at*

---

[37] *The Complete Edgar Cayce Readings*, Document #51704, 4905-002 Reports, letter to Cayce from Mr. Gumbinsky dated 8/26/24.

Mischief. He said that his sleeping subject never knew what he said when he was in the subconscious state and unless he was told subsequently, never knew that he had been used. If Cayce were the sleeping subject, perhaps he was never told! How could I prove this? An interesting discovery led me to the verification of this deduction, and will be discussed later in reference to Sir Hubert Wilkins.

5. Use of Existing Texts

The Urantia Book contains considerable portions of text that can be identified as previously published literary works composed by other authors.[38] Some of the books identified as source books for Urantia material were printed in *The Spiritual Fellowship Journal* in 1993:

> *The Ways of the Gods*, 1905
> *The Theology of Personality*, 1926
> *The Dawn of Conscience*, 1933
> *The Religion of Jesus*, 1928
> *Our Recovery of Jesus*, 1929
> *The Life of Christ*, 1900, 1927
> *Human Biology and Racial Welfare*, 1930
> *The New Dictionary of Thoughts*, 1890-1934
> *The Hope of the World*, 1933
> *The Sacred Writings of the World's Great Religions*, 1943
> *Man's Vision of God*, 1941
> *Origin and Evolution of Religion*, 1923
> *A Preface to Christian Faith in the New Age*, 1932
> *The Inner Life*, 1916
> *Purposive Evolution: The Link Between Science and Evolution*, 1926
> *Man Rises to Parnasus: Critical Epochs in the Prehistory of Man*, 1928
> *The Autobiography of a Philosopher*, 1930
> *Religions of Authority and the Religion of the Spirit*, 1904
> *The Architecture of the Universe*, 1934

---

[38] Martin Gardner, *Urantia: The Great Cult Mystery* (Amherst, NY: Prometheus, 1995) Chap. 16.

My next question was, "Did Cayce ever recommend books to people while he was in a trance?"

If so, I reasoned that he could have recommended books to Sadler. I discovered that in the readings, Cayce *did* suggest books while unconscious. I learned that a person needed only to ask Cayce and he could identify the books that should be studied to locate the information that was sought. Cayce would identify the book and/or author. Illustrated in the following examples are two instances of Cayce's ability to suggest books and authors during the readings, given in different years:

Q. Do you know of any books better than those of T.J.J. See regarding etheonic etc.? [see 440-11 Reports, Par. R31 -- R34 in re T.J.J.]
A. As we find in general, there has been little approach to the subject better than these, but much of a background for the proper understanding of that being presented here is necessary - that may be gained in relation to the influences of the outside world, or in "this Mysterious Universe" or the like, see? [Our Mysterious Universe by Sir James Jeans][39], 1934.

Q. Give a list of scientific books for me to study during the coming year, especially during the next three months, relating to this subject?
A. First we would suggest "This Mysterious World of Ours." [The Mysterious Universe by Sir James Jeans?][40], 1933.

Since the list of Urantia source books appeared in *The Spiritual Fellowship Journal*,[41] Matthew Block has compiled an enormous list of books used in the Urantia text. He plans to

---

[39] *The Complete Edgar Cayce Readings*, Document #13078, 0440-011 Text, (1/9/34).

[40] *The Complete Edgar Cayce Readings*, Document #13062, 0440-007 Text, (12/21/33).

[41] Published by the Fort Wayne Society of Students of *The Urantia Book*, Fort Wayne, IN.

publish his findings when his work is complete. Many of the books and/or authors that Matthew has identified as source books for *The Urantia Book* can be found in the A.R.E. library holdings. (One source book for *The Urantia Book* is *The Universe Around Us*, 1929, by Sir James Jeans, the same author recommended by Cayce in the above readings!)

One implication suggested by this is the possibility that significant portions of the Urantia text could have originated from *source books* suggested by Cayce during a trance, rather than coming directly through him. *The Urantia Book* itself says that over a thousand human concepts were used from mortals of the past and present.[42] This sheds some light on the puzzle of how a 2,000-page book could have been channeled by a man as busy and distant as Cayce.

This also suggests an explanation to part of the mystery concerning the differences in the way the subject matter is expressed in the Cayce readings compared to text of *The Urantia Book*.

There is one other discovery that seems noteworthy. About one hundred years before the events that occurred with Dr. Sadler's sleeping subject, another doctor had a sleeping subject who spoke while unconscious, which resulted in a huge volume titled *The Principles of Nature, Her Divine Revelations, and a Voice to Mankind*. The information that was spoken by the unconscious man, was recorded by a stenographer and later published in 1846. The doctor claimed that except for grammar and punctuation, he made no changes to the text. The book claims flatly to be a revelation. See Appendix F for a list of words and ideas from that book which parallel the Cayce readings and The Urantia Book.

---

[42] *The Urantia Book*, 17.

6. Cayce in Chicago

One thing I wanted to know was, "How often was Cayce in Chicago?" I knew from reading *There is a River:* that he had made a trip to Chicago for ten days once in 1911.[43] But that wouldn't possibly have given him time to complete the Urantia project.

So thought Dr. Jacques Rheaume, a former Catholic priest who now is a professor in Quebec, Canada. In his 700 page doctoral thesis, written in French for the University of Ottawa in 1983, he wrote:

> The information coming through the subject was both written and oral but that's all the information Dr. Sadler gave about it. The man talked during his sleep - and remembered nothing of what happened when he awoke. One can think of Edgar Cayce, who matches this description. But as the contact group always worked in Chicago and since Cayce traveled so much over the years, we can rule him out despite certain resemblances.[44]

However, with further investigation I located documents in *The Complete Edgar Cayce Readings* on CD-ROM, which placed Cayce in Chicago during 1911, 1923, 1924, 1925, 1927, 1928, 1930, 1931, 1932, 1933, 1934, 1937, and 1939. These were the years that *The Urantia Book* was compiled.

I have listed 80 references to him being in Chicago in Appendix C, sometimes as long as three weeks. There were also numerous references to his planning trips to Chicago. He may have made other trips there, but because the A.R.E. records are incomplete we can never know for sure.

---

[43] Sugrue, 164.

[44] Jacques Rheaume, "Analysis of a Revealed Text: *The Urantia Book*," diss., University of Ottawa, 1983, 32.

One month prior to Cayce's trip to Chicago, in a reading dated 2/13/11, the forces speaking through him seem to be having a discussion amongst themselves.

"We have contact here with the material world."

"Whereby or how, shall we gain the material means for furtherance of the ethereal project here?"

"We establish credence with the material [world]."

Providing verifiable medical diagnoses and treatments was the means for them to establish confidence in the minds of mortal men. They described Edgar Cayce as the 'concourse' (or crossroads) for communication between the material and spiritual planes of existence. [45]

Newspapers began to print stories about Edgar Cayce as early as 1901. His was an ability to impart information while in an unconscious state of trance that appeared to be normal sleep.

The information imparted through him did not parallel the activity of his conscious mind, his habit of thought, or the way he had been taught. Much of the information that came through Cayce was contrary to his religious upbringing.[46] Cayce's periods of trance that occurred from time to time were not séances.   Dr. Sadler made these same statements when describing the sleeping subject.

In October 1922, the Birmingham *Age-Herald* newspaper ran an article in which Cayce is quoted as saying: "No; I do not believe in spiritualism but I do believe in spirituality."[47]

---

[45] *The Complete Edgar Cayce Readings*, Document #3778, 0254-001 Text, (2/13/11).

[46] Jeffrey Furst, *Edgar Cayce's Story of Jesus* (New York: Coward-McCann, 1969) 10.

[47] David M. Leary, *Edgar Cayce's Photographic Legacy* (New York: Doubleday, 1978) 86.

Edgar Cayce communicated with a higher source of universal consciousness, which encompassed all subconscious minds.

7. The Stock Market Connection

Dr. Sadler referred to the sleeping subject as a stockbroker. How could this refer to Cayce?

Cayce invented a game about the stock market called 'Pit'. It was marketed and became a popular game. This fact, combined with Cayce's ability to predict the stock market and speak the jargon of stockbrokers while in a trance may be why (if the sleeping subject was Cayce) Dr. Sadler referred to him as a stockbroker.

In *There is a River:*, the author writes, "Edgar, who listened every evening at the dinner table to discussions of the wheat market in Chicago, worked out something he called 'Pit' or 'Board of Trade'."[48]

Edgar Cayce's Photographic Legacy, by David M. Leary, contains news articles on the story of 'The Pit' and 'New Parlor Game' as reported by two different newspapers, printed about the year 1903. It was a game about "the various cereals, railroad, mining stock, etc., which are sold by the New York exchange," and "copies of the Pit or Board of Trade, the parlor game invented by Edgar Cayce of this city have been received by the Bookstores of Bowling Green and are in big demand."[49]

---

[48] Sugrue, 119.
[49] Leary, 32.

8. Historical Points of Interest

Ancient Mesopotamian Cities

The Urantia Book includes mention of Sumerian and Egyptian civilizations, as do the Cayce readings. When I realized this, I decided to make a list of all the ancient cities in the Sumerian region. Then I looked up every city *in The Urantia Book* and in the Cayce readings. I discovered that various ancient Mesopotamian cities were mentioned or left out in a striking parallel. The proportion of inclusion and omission of cities between *The Urantia Book* and the Cayce readings surprised me. These ancient cities are listed in Appendix E.

Bud Bromley (a retired college math professor) and I had been producing a television show about *The Urantia Book* for five years. One day at the television studio, I gave my manuscript to him to read. A couple of weeks later he telephoned me and he sounded excited. He explained that he had conducted a mathematics test, called the Coefficient of Correlation, on the lists of the ancient cities. After viewing the results of the test, Bud said that there is a correlation of $R=0.996+$ (a perfect correlation would be $R=1.0$).

He said, "It is highly probable, highly isn't a strong enough word, that some one factor caused the similarity of both lists. The odds of this happening randomly are trillions to one. There is no possibility of random chance."

The Three Concentric Circles

The symbol used for *The Urantia Book* is three concentric circles. Where did this symbol originate? The answers that I discovered surprised me!

The circles were a diagram of the ringed city of Atlantis, reported by Plato. According to Plato, Poseidon shaped the city

area around his home into three concentric circles of land.[50]
(The Cayce readings state that Atlantis was an actual prehistoric
city. The readings contain abundant information about the
ancient Atlantean civilization.)

The diagram of the ringed city of Atlantis and the symbol
used for Urantia are the same. Each diagram or symbol
coincides with the three concentric circles of the Zodiac, which
originated somewhere in antiquity.

Ancient Symbol of the Universe[51]

Ancient symbolism, as I discovered in the *Encyclopedia of
the Celts*[52], used three concentric circles to represent God and
the universe. The totality of being as it now exists is represented

---

[50] Shirley Andrews, Atlantis: *Insights from a Lost Civilization*   (St. Paul,
Minn.: Llewellyn Publications, 1997) 117.

[51] Reproduced from "The Chart of Symbols: Symbols from Ancient Times to
the Middle Ages," copyrighted wall chart from The Catalpa Tree Shops in
Grabill, IN.

[52] Wright, David. "Encyclopaedia of the Celts: Glastonbury - God and
Cythrawl." < http://www.ealaghol.demon.co.uk/celtenc/celt_g2.htm>
(4/10/99). Excerpts from *Encyclopaedia of the Celts*, compiled & edited
by Knud Mariboe, 1994.

by these circles. The innermost of them is called 'Abred' and is the stage of struggle and evolution. The next is the circle of 'Gwynfyd', or Purity, in which life is manifested as a pure, rejoicing force, having attained its triumph over evil. The last and outermost circle is called 'Ceugant', or infinity.

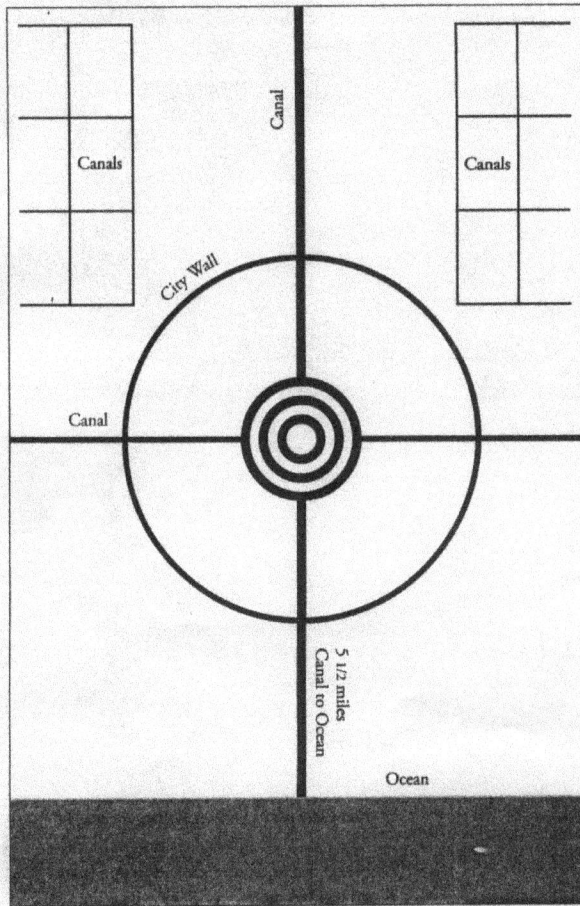

Diagram of the Ringed City of Atlantis

Part II. The People Involved

1. Introduction

The tangled web of interactions between the different play-ers in this story makes it difficult to clearly illustrate how every-one came together. It could rival any mystery novel for its complexity and surprising associations. The main personalities were, of course, William Sadler (person in charge of the Urantia Revelation) and Edgar Cayce (well-known psychic). The next layer of significant individuals are those known to have associated with both of them, namely Harold Sherman, William Randolph Hearst, Harry Houdini, and Mrs. 3316 (who's letter was included in the opening paragraphs of this book). The big surprise came with the discovery of Sir Hubert Wilkins, an Arctic explorer who was involved in a quiet way with *The Urantia Book*, and inadvertently solved one of the greatest puzzles in the whole story.

Dates of Births and Deaths

NAME	DOB	DOD	AGE AT DEATH
Edgar Cayce	1877	1945	67
William Sadler	1875	1969	93
William Hearst	1863	1951	89
Howard Thurston	1869	1936	67
Harry Houdini	1874	1926	52
Roswell Field	1851	1919	68
George Wilkins	1888	1958	70
Wilfred Kellogg	1876	1956	80
Harold Sherman	1898	1987	89
Harry Loose	1869*	1943	74*

*estimated

People Involved with Sadler and Cayce

This is an illustration of people involved with Dr. Sadler and the Urantia manuscript. I am attempting to show the saturation of level of Cayce into the lives of Dr. Sadler's associates. It is my intent to show you that everyone around Sadler was familiar with Cayce.

SADLER & ASSOCIATES	PERSONS INVOLVED WITH CAYCE
Dr. William Sadler was involved with:	Mrs. 3316 (Forum Member) – involved with Cayce
	Harold Sherman (Forum Member) – involved with Cayce
	Sir Hubert Wilkins -- involved with Hearst who was involved with Cayce
	Harry Houdini -- involved with Cayce
	Harry Loose – involved with Sherman – involved with Cayce
Dr. Lena Sadler was involved with: (wife of William Sadler)	Mrs. 3316 (Forum Member) – involved with Cayce
	Harold Sherman (Forum Member) – involved with Cayce
	Sir Hubert Wilkins -- involved with Hearst who was involved with Cayce
	Harry Houdini -- involved with Cayce
Bill Sadler, Jr. was involved with: (son of William Sadler)	Mrs. 3316 (Forum Member) – involved with Cayce
	Harold Sherman (Forum Member) – involved with Cayce
	Sir Hubert Wilkins -- involved with Hearst who was involved with Cayce

SADLER & ASSOCIATES	PERSONS INVOLVED WITH CAYCE
Emma Christensen was involved with: (Sadler's adopted daughter, Christy)	Mrs. 3316 (Forum Member) – involved with Cayce
	Harold Sherman (Forum Member) -- involved with Cayce
	Sir Hubert Wilkins -- involved with Hearst who was involved with Cayce
Nola Smith[53] Handwriting expert, Forum member	Friend of Dr. Sadler Employed by Bill Sadler, Jr. Member of Cayce's A.R.E. 1940's
Wilfred Kellogg was involved with: (brother-in-law to William Sadler) (cousin to Lena Kellogg)	Mrs. 3316 (Forum Member) – involved with Cayce
	Harold Sherman (Forum Member) -- involved with Cayce
	Sir Hubert Wilkins -- involved with Hearst who was involved with Cayce
	Harry Houdini -- involved with Cayce
Anna Kellogg was involved with: (wife of Wilfred Kellogg) (cousin of Wilfred Kellogg) (sister of Lena Kellogg)	Mrs. 3316 (Forum Member) – involved with Cayce
	Harold Sherman (Forum Member) -- involved with Cayce
	Sir Hubert Wilkins -- involved with Hearst who was involved with Cayce
	Harry Houdini -- involved with Cayce

---

[53] Per telephone conversation between the authors and Nola Smith on 6/6/99.

Dr. William S. Sadler

2. William S. Sadler

William Samuel Sadler left home at an early age and arrived in Battle Creek, Michigan, where he found employment at the Kellogg Sanitarium. The Sanitarium was founded and operated by Dr. John Harvey Kellogg. Sadler admired Kellogg and they became close associates. While employed at the Sanitarium, Sadler met Lena Kellogg, Dr. Kellogg's niece. During his association with Kellogg, Sadler began to study medicine, married Lena, moved to Chicago, and together he and his new wife graduated medical school in 1906.[54] Upon his graduation, Sadler announced his intention to write books and become a public speaker so that he could carry the message of health to the public.[55] The American Medical Association, however, had a strict rule against advertising and they considered public speaking by any doctor to be a form of advertising.[56]

There was an organization that operated its headquarters in Chicago, called the Redpath Lyceum and Chautauqua Bureau. Lyceums were public gatherings where speakers would entertain public audiences with talks on various topics. In the early years, during the mid-1800's, the meetings were held at public buildings or in churches. (Mark Twain was a well-known author and lecturer for the Lyceum, but he didn't like speaking in churches.) Later, Lyceums were held in tents and adopted the name Chautauqua from Lake Chautauqua, New York, where the first "Chautauqua" meeting was held. Traveling Chautauquas took to the road in 1904.

Sadler was a member of the International Mark Twain Society. Perhaps his admiration of Twain helped to spark his interest in becoming a lecturer for Chautauqua. He gave his first speech in 1905. After graduating medical school in 1906,

---

[54] G. Vonne Meussling, "William S. Sadler: Chautauqua's Medic Orator," diss., Bowling Green State University, 1970, 27-28.
[55] Meussling, 8-10, 167-68.
[56] Meussling, 1.

he traveled to cities away from Chicago, on the Chautauqua circuit, to give public talks about health.

Locomotives were the common mode of travel for Chautauqua speakers. The L&N Railroad Line linked Chicago to Hopkinsville, Kentucky[57] and to other cities in Dixie Land. The small town of Hopkinsville was Edgar Cayce's hometown and had a Lyceum complete with weekly lectures beginning in 1831.[58] Hopkinsville was fortunate enough to be located in one of the best areas of Kentucky, with a moral, energetic, and intelligent population alive to improvements of every kind.

A Chautauqua tent was first established in Hopkinsville in 1905.[59]

Sadler's interest in medicine and spiritualism expanded into the study of the human psyche, which led him to establish the Chicago Institute of Research and Diagnosis in 1909. His research led him into the investigation of psychics, mediums, and the occult, which in turn contributed to his pursuit of psychiatry. From 1909 to 1929, Dr. Sadler devoted a great deal of time and effort to the study of psychic phenomenon at his institute.

His investigations (which began during the late 1800's) had convinced him that all psychic phenomena were either fraudulent or due to tricks of the subconscious mind, until in 1906 he met the man who channeled the Urantia information and, in 1911, began to study him.

During the years following 1911, Dr. Sadler conducted his medical business as usual, treating patients for various medical problems. He had been expanding his medical interests into the

----

[57] William Turner, Historian for Christian Co., Ky., provided this information and the photograph included on page 88.

[58] Carl Bode, *The American Lyceum-Town Meeting of the Mind* (New York: Oxford University Press, 1956) 82.

[59] Per conversation with D.D. Cayce, III, Hopkinsville, KY.

field of psychiatry, and thus could offer advice to patients to help them improve their thinking, in addition to treating their physical conditions. Sadler realized that a healthy mind contributed to a healthy body. His background and involvement with the Kellogg Institute in Battle Creek had taught him to understand the importance of healthy eating and proper exercise. But his interest in psychiatry taught him to understand the importance of healthy thinking.

Articles written by Dr. Sadler began to appear in newspapers and magazines and it wasn't long before his books began to be published. His manuscript, *The Mind at Mischief,* was published in 1929. In the Appendix, he told the story of meeting the contact person for *The Urantia Book* in 1911, which may have been Cayce, although he did not mention him by name.

44

3. Sadler Writes about the Sleeping Subject

The Mind at Mischief discusses abnormal phenomenon of the subconscious mind, including the paranormal. Throughout the book, whenever he makes references to the sleeping subject of the Urantia Papers, Sadler refers the reader to the Appendix. Following are several of those references, with some noteworthy parallels to the Cayce story included:

> Preface, page VII: I have been afforded an opportunity, in association with my colleagues in the Chicago Institute of Research and Diagnosis, to observe, over a period of twenty years, a large number of men and women who were sufferers from various personality disturbances as well as a large number of clairvoyants, physics, automatic writers, trance mediums, etc.

> Page 267: The reader is referred to the Appendix for brief notice of a very unusual case of supposedly automatic writing associated with other psychic phenomena which came under my observation many years ago.

[Two readings on the *Complete Edgar Cayce Readings* on CD-ROM insinuate that Cayce sometimes wrote during his sleep trances.[60] Doris Agee, in her book *Edgar Cayce on ESP*, refers to Cayce as the sleeping editor.[61]]

> Page 332: ... it is my opinion that the vast majority of those who have made such supernatural claims were either out-and-out frauds or self-deceived individuals, who, in their ignorance of things psychical, actually believed their spells, visions, or visitations to be of divine origin. As far as my actual experience goes -- as far as I have personally been able to test

----

[60] *The Complete Edgar Cayce Readings*, Document #3830, 0254-014 Text, (10/27/24) and Document #45026, 3744-002 Text, (10/9/23).
[61] Agee, 67.

and observe those who have seizures or experiences of this sort -- I have not yet met with a case in which I could not, after a thoroughgoing examination, discover certain psychic, chemical, and physical influences which quite fully accounted -- at least to my own satisfaction -- for their extraordinary behavior.

Perhaps this statement should be qualified by adding that there are possibly one or two exceptions to this general classification of so-called psychics and trance mediums. Many years ago I was made acquainted with a very extraordinary phenomenon of this sort, which it has been my privilege to observe periodically from that time to this...

[Sadler observed the sleeping subject periodically from 1911 to the publication of his book in 1929, and beyond. Cayce was in Chicago periodically during those and subsequent years.]

... and someday I hope to report more fully on this unique case; but I hasten to say that in none of my observations of this individual and the peculiar associated experiences of the night period was there ever anything that pointed toward spiritualism. In fact, the contacts of this individual with the alleged forces which dominated at such times, whatever they were, were always in a most positive manner antagonistic to, and condemnatory of, all beliefs or tendencies associated with the idea of the return of the dead to participate in the affairs of the world of the living.

[The forces speaking through the sleeping Cayce were always, in a most positive manner, condemnatory of the idea of contact of the living with departed human beings and advised against it.]

Page 352: Again I must record that I have come in contact with a few individuals of psychic peculiarity, who were the channel of communication for numerous messages that were not of a trivial nature; but in no instance did these messages lay claim to have had their origin with deceased human

beings. They always claimed an origin separate and apart
from the realm of departed spirits.

[Cayce and his associates were convinced that discarnate
personalities were not giving his readings.[62] Cayce based none
of his work on communication with the dead.[63]]

Appendix of *The Mind at Mischief*

Dr. Sadler's Appendix is reproduced word for word for those
who do not possess a copy of that book. I have made some
comments about Cayce where they seemed applicable,
therefore the text of the Appendix is in bold type.

**In discussions of fraudulent mediums or
self-deceived psychics, the reader of this book has
several times encountered the statement that there
were certain exceptions to the general indictments
there made, and was referred to this Appendix. It
now becomes my duty to explain what I had in
mind when those footnotes were inserted.**

**In the interest of scientific accuracy on the one
hand, and of strict fairness on the other, it becomes
necessary to explain that there are one or two exceptions to the general statement that all cases of
psychic phenomena which have come under my observation have turned out to be those of auto-psy-
chism. It is true that practically all the physical
phenomena have proved to be fraudulent, while the
psychic phenomena are almost invariably explain-
able by the laws of psychic projection, transference,
reality shifting, etc. But many years ago I did meet**

---

[62] Bro, *Edgar Cayce on Religion and Psychic Experience*, 29.
[63] Bro, *Edgar Cayce on Religion and Psychic Experience*, 18.

one trance medium, a woman now deceased, whose visions, revelations, etc., were not tainted with spiritualism. As far as my knowledge extends, at no time did she claim to be under the influence of spirit guides or controls, or to communicate messages from the spirits of departed human beings. Her work was largely of a religious nature and consisted of elevated sayings and religious admonitions. I never had the privilege of making a thoroughgoing psychic analysis of this case, and am not in a position to express myself as to the extent to which her revelations originated in the subconscious realms of her own mind. I make mention of the case merely to record the fact that I have met one instance of psychic phenomena apparently of the trance order that was not in any way associated with spiritualism.

The above is believed to be a reference to Ellen White.

The other exception has to do with a rather peculiar case of psychic phenomena, one which I find myself unable to classify, and which I would like very much to narrate more fully; I cannot do so here, however, because of a promise which I feel under obligation to keep sacredly. In other words, I have promised not to publish this case during the lifetime of the individual.

Could this promise be a reference to the code of professional ethics governing confidentiality? Many people say "No." However, I notice the way in which Sadler expressed himself concerning the promise; it was not a sacred promise, but a promise he felt he must keep sacredly. Some people may have interpreted the use of the word "sacred" to imply that it was a divine promise. Consequently, this may have given rise to the belief that Sadler made a sacred promise to divine beings that he would never reveal the human's identity, because the divine beings wanted to keep it a secret.

Dr. Sadler goes on to explain, "In other words, I have promised not to publish this case during the lifetime of the individual." When Sadler restated his promise, no association with divinity was expressed. Edgar Cayce died in 1945, ten years prior to the publication of *The Urantia Book*.

> **I hope sometime to secure a modification of that promise and to be able to report this case more fully because of its interesting features. I was brought in contact with it, in the summer of 1911,**

"Edgar was invited to visit Chicago as a guest of the Hearst papers. He went early in March 1911, along with his father and Mr. Noe, and stayed for ten days, meeting people, giving readings, and answering the most preposterous questions he had ever heard."[64] Sadler recalls that it was *summer* when he met the contact person, but he was remembering it 18 years later, so it is possible the season of the year may have been spring.

> **and I have had it under my observation more or less ever since, having been present at probably 250 of the night sessions...**

Readings given after 6:00 p.m. are documented in at least 238 readings on the Cayce CD-ROM, some as late as 11:45 p.m.

In her book *Many Mansions*, Gina Cerminara said readings could be given at night or any time.[65] Why were Sadler's sessions held exclusively at night? Was it because during the day there was the usual medical business to conduct with paying customers? Perhaps the evenings afforded the only practical time.

---

[64] Sugrue, 163-4.
[65] Cerminara, 19.

... many of which have been attended by a stenographer who took voluminous notes.

There was also a stenographer present during Cayce's readings. If the sleeping subject had written the Urantia Papers, as some accounts suggest, there would have been no need for a stenographer.

A thorough study of this case has convinced me that it is not one of ordinary trance. While the sleep seems to be quite of a natural order, it is very profound, and so far we have never been able to awaken this subject when in this state; ...

In *There is a River:*, Sugrue states that in 1901 an osteopath named Layne described Edgar's sleep state as "a self-imposed hypnotic trance which induces clairvoyance."[66] It was impossible for Edgar Cayce to be awakened from a trance unless he was given a command to awaken by the voice of the person who had given him the hypnotic suggestion to enter the trance state. When in this trance state, he was oblivious to pain and all external stimuli.

"His family and staff well knew that there had been times when it had been impossible to waken Cayce from his trance state, when none of the hypnotic suggestions worked and when the passing hours were marked by his flagging respiration."[67]

... but the body is never rigid, and the heart action is never modified, though respiration is sometimes markedly interfered with. The man is utterly unconscious, wholly oblivious to what takes place,

---

[66] Sugrue, 121,127.
[67] Bro, *Edgar Cayce on Religion and Psychic Experience*, 21.

Over the years, various doctors had administered different methods in attempting to awaken him. Some of these were:

sticking a hat pin completely through his cheeks,

sticking him with pins,

probing beneath his fingernail with a pocket knife,

pouring whiskey down his throat,

prying his mouth open and in the process breaking a couple lower front teeth,

injecting him with morphine,

injecting him with strychnine,

placing hot stove lids against the bottoms of his feet.[68]

A letter from Dr. Wesley H. Ketchum, MD, dated 1910, to the American Association of Clinical Research, describes Edgar Cayce: "While in this sleep, which to all intents and purposes is a natural sleep, his objective mind is completely inactive and only his subjective [mind] is working."

The Cayce readings state:

...When [the] physical or mental, material or mental are subjugated like this body here we are speaking of, Edgar Cayce, the physical is subjugated or laid aside, we find the soul forces give the information, and the body is under the subjugation of the soul and spirit forces.[69]

"... The personality is removed from the individual, and only that other forces in the trinity occupying the body and using only its elements to communicate as in this body here, we have spoken of. With the submerging of the conscious to

---

[68] Sugrue, 130-33, 137-38.

[69] *The Complete Edgar Cayce Readings*, Document #45026, 3744-002 Text, #17 (10/9/23).

the subconscious, the personality of the body or earthly portions are removed and lie above the other body."[70]

In *There is a River:*, Sugrue recounts a conversation that took place when Dr. Hugo Munsterberg was investigating Cayce:

> "When you are asleep you know everything. Is that it?"
> "That's what they tell me," [said Cayce]. "I don't know."[71]

... and unless told about it subsequently never knows that he has been used as a sort of clearing house for the coming and going of alleged extra-planetary personalities.

Hugh Lynn Cayce says about his father, "It should be kept in mind that Edgar Cayce was never consciously aware of anything he said while giving a psychic reading. In other words he was functioning at an unconscious level."[72]

On March 29, 1904, a story appeared in a Nashville, Tenn. paper which stated: "Cayce remembers nothing he has said when he comes out of the trance, and it is all a perfect blank to him." (This, combined with the secrecy embraced by the Urantia participants, may be the main reason no one ever made a connection between the two cases.)

Some messages came through him from other entities and when so, it was announced by Edgar Cayce in his own voice that this message was being relayed from so and so.[73] Although Cayce spoke in his own voice, the tone and volume of his voice was stronger and the speech was characteristically different from the awakened Edgar Cayce's mannerism.

---

[70] *The Complete Edgar Cayce Readings*, Document #45026, 3744-002 Text, #23 (10/9/23).
[71] Sugrue, 13-14.
[72] Cayce, *Venture Inward*, 41.
[73] *The Complete Edgar Cayce Readings*, Document #57044, 5756-001 Reports, (11/1/24).

In fact, he is more or less indifferent to the whole proceeding, and shows a surprising lack of interest in these affairs as they occur from time to time.

An example of Cayce's passive disinterest to the procedure of psychic readings is illustrated in *There is a River:*, regarding readings he gave to Dr. Wesley Ketchum for medical patients: "During the visits he [Cayce] had gone to [Dr.] Ketchum's office each day, given readings, asked no questions, and requested only the assurance that the cases were all people in need of help."[74]

Regarding the human contact, *The Urantia Book* says: "... it is indeed fortunate that he remains consciously quite unconcerned about the entire procedure. He holds one of the highly experienced Adjusters of his day and generation, and yet his passive reaction to, and inactive concern toward, the phenomena associated with the presence in his mind of this versatile Adjuster is pronounced by the guardian of destiny to be a rare and fortuitous reaction."[75]

In no way are these night visitations like the seances associated with spiritualism. At no time during the period of eighteen years' observation has there been a communication from any source that claimed to be the spirit of a deceased human being.

Cayce in no way wanted his spirituality confused with spiritualism and made a point of saying so.[76] His readings were not like seances, in fact he condemned seances. He discouraged

---

[74] Sugrue, 153.
[75] *The Urantia Book*, 1209.
[76] Leary, 86.

people from seeking to contact departed human beings and suggested rather that they seek God. In *Edgar Cayce's Story of
Jesus*, Jeffrey Furst makes this clear, saying, "within the readings, he continually warned against communication with the
dead--and all such occupations as automatic writing, seances,
and ouija boards."[77]

The communications which have been written...

One reading refers to articles written by Cayce while in the
trance state.[78]   Another reading describes the process of
reducing psychic messages to writing:

> "The personality is that as known on the physical plane in the
> subconscious or when the subconscious controls, the person-
> ality is removed from the individual, and only that other forces
> in the trinity occupying the body and using only its elements
> to communicate as in this body here, we have spoken of. With
> the submerging of the conscious to the subconscious, the
> personality of the body or earthly portions are removed and
> lie above the other body. They may be seen here. Hence the
> disturbing of those conditions bring distress to the other
> portions of the entity or individual. With the return then we
> find the personality leaves those impressions with those
> portions of the body, as we have given for the *arm force* here,
> you see."[79] [emphasis mine]

**... or which we have had the opportunity to hear
spoken, are made by a vast order of alleged beings
who claim to come from other planets to visit this
world to stop here as student visitors for study and**

---

[77] Furst, 302.
[78] *The Complete Edgar Cayce Readings*, Document #3830, 0254-014 Text,
     (10/27/24).
[79] *The Complete Edgar Cayce Readings*, Document #45026, 3744-002 Text,
     (10/9/23).

**observation when they are en route from one uni-
verse to another or from one planet to another.**

Documents contained within the A.R.E. reveal that Cayce
spoke with "celestial visitors". The information given during
the readings tell of the vastness of creation and of other planets,
other spheres of existence, and other universes.

Cayce said, "As a matter of fact, there would seem to be not
only one, but several sources of information I tap when in this
sleeping condition.[80]

> ... the information is obtained through that connection be-
> tween subconscious soul or spirit forces as directed, and di-
> rected to. Suggestions being that manner in which the
> direction is given. Hence how the reflections, either direct or
> wavered, are obtained, just as the subconscious force of the
> director is held in that direction the information is obtained
> and in the same manner that it, the director's subconscious
> wavers, the reflections become in the same manner wavered.[81]

> ... the source may be from the subconscious forces of the body
> itself, or from the realm of spirit force as may surround the
> body, or a combination of both; or from a universal con-
> sciousness that is the source of life itself, and worded, when
> worded, in a manner by the forces of creation, or of the higher
> orders themselves; and the variation dependent upon that,
> when worded, as to the attitude of the one seeking and of that
> sought.

> These sources may be more clearly understood by dividing
> them as follows:
> 　　The subconscious mind of Edgar Cayce.
> 　　The subconscious minds of other individuals in the earth
> 　　　plane.

---

[80] Furst, 15.

[81] *The Complete Edgar Cayce Readings*, Document #45026, 3744-002 Text,
(10/9/23).

> The subconscious minds of discarnate entities in the spirit
> plane in any of the spheres of development.
> The soul minds of higher orders themselves.
> The akashic records.
> The universal or pure cosmic consciousness.[82]

Edgar Cayce's mind is amenable to suggestion, the same as all other subconscious minds, but in addition thereto it has the power to interpret to the objective mind of others what it acquires from the subconscious mind of other individuals of the same kind. The subconscious mind forgets nothing. The conscious mind receives the impression from without and transfers all thought to the subconscious, where it remains even though the conscious be destroyed.[83]

The Urantia Book indicates that some of its information came from human sources. "We have selected as the basis for these papers more than one thousand human concepts ... from ... mortals ... of the past and the present."[84] This may correlate to the Cayce source "of discarnate entities in the spirit plane in any sphere of development."[85]

These communications further arise in alleged spiritual beings who purport to have been assigned to this planet for duties of various sorts.

Eighteen years of study and careful investigation have failed to reveal the psychic origin of these messages. I find myself at the present time just where I was when I started. Psychoanalysis, hyp-notism, intensive comparison, fail to show that the

---

[82] *The Complete Edgar Cayce Readings*, Document #8360, 0294-131 Reports, (1/25/32).

[83] *The Complete Edgar Cayce Readings*, Document #57044, 5756-001 Reports, (11/1/24).

[84] *The Urantia Book*, 17.

[85] *The Complete Edgar Cayce Readings*, Document #4028, 0254-063 Reports, (4/26/32).

written or spoken messages of this individual have origin in his own mind.

The readings state:

> This realm from which such information is obtainable, as we have given, is either from those that have passed into the realm of subconscious activity or from the subconscious and superconscious activity through which information is being sought by that superconscious activity in the realm of physical forces in action. Hence why this particular body, Edgar Cayce, was able to attune self to the varied realms of activity by laying aside the physical consciousness.[86]
> In this state the conscious mind becomes subjugated to the subconscious, superconscious or soul mind; and may and does communicate with like minds, and the subconscious or soul force becomes universal.[87]

> The subconscious mind of Edgar Cayce is in direct communication with all other subconscious minds, and is capable of interpreting through his objective mind and imparting impressions received to other objective minds, gathering in this way all knowledge possessed by *millions of other subconscious minds*[88] [emphasis mine]

Much of the material secured through this subject is quite contrary to his habits of thought, the way in which he has been taught, and to his entire philosophy.

---

[86] *The Complete Edgar Cayce Readings*, Document #57094, 5756-014 Text, (7/17/34).
[87] *The Complete Edgar Cayce Readings*, Document #45026, 3744-002 Text, (10/9/23).
[88] *The Complete Edgar Cayce Readings*, Document #57044, 5756-001 Reports, (11/1/24).

Author Jeffrey Furst states: "The paradox exists in the fact that much of the information which came through the sleeping Cayce was extremely alien to the awakened Edgar Cayce's manner of thinking -- and especially contrary to his fundamentalist Christian background."[89]

Dr. Gina Cerminara comments that "Cayce's inner turmoil is not difficult to understand. He had been brought up in a strict atmosphere of orthodox Christianity."[90]

In fact, of much that we have secured, we have failed to find anything of its nature in existence. Its philosophic content is quite new, and we are unable to find where very much of it has found human expression.

Much as I would like to report details of this case, I am not in a position to do so at present. I can only say that I have found in these years of observation that all the information imparted through this source has proved to be consistent within itself.

Dr. Cerminara evaluates information coming through the sleeping Edgar Cayce: "The data was self-consistent over a period of twenty-two years; that is to say, it agreed with itself, both in basic content and minute detail, in hundreds of separate readings taken at different times."[91]

While there is considerable difference in the quality of the communications ...

If there were "considerable differences in the quality of the communications," why doesn't *The Urantia Book* reflect this?

---

[89] Furst, 10.
[90] Cerminara, 33.
[91] Cerminara, 238.

**...this seems to be reasonably explained by a differ-
ence in state of development and order of personalities making the communications.**

The Cayce readings indicate that there are a number of reasons why the quality of the communications would differ. The
attitudes of the people present, the physical condition of Cayce,
the mind of the person asking questions, and the environment
were all factors which contributed to the quality of the communications.

**Its philosophy is consistent. It is essentially Chris-
tian and is, on the whole, entirely harmonious with
the known scientific facts and truths of this age.**

Dr. Cerminara said that the Cayce readings were consistent
in every detail throughout his life.[92] "But above all, the Cayce
readings achieve a synthesis between science and religion."[93]

Cayce's family and associates distinguished carefully what
was said by the waking Cayce and what was said by "the information," as they called the unknown source or sources of his
trances. They viewed these sources as inclusive of Cayce, yet
independent, intelligent, impersonal, and in keeping with Biblical faith.[94]

**In fact the case is so unusual and extraordinary
that it establishes itself immediately, as far as my
experience goes, in a class by itself, one that has
thus far resisted all my efforts to prove it to be of
auto-psychic origin. Our investigations are being**

---

[92] Cerminara, 238.
[93] Cerminara, 45.
[94] Bro, *Edgar Cayce on Religion and Psychic Experience*, 21.

continued and, as I have intimated, I hope sometime in the near future to secure permission for the
more complete reporting of the phenomena connected with this interesting case.

[end Appendix]

60

The Redpath Chautauqua Special Enroute from Chicago to Dixie Land 1913

The Chautauqua Express at the Hopkinsville Train Station[95]

---

[95] William Turner, Historian for Christian Co., Ky., provided this photograph.

4. When Did Sadler Become Involved with Cayce?

On the previous page is a photograph of the Chautauqua train from Chicago, parked at the train station in Hopkinsville in 1913. The first Chautauqua tent was erected there in 1905, one year before Dr. Sadler graduated from medical school and began his lecturing career. Dr. Sadler had the means and the motive to be in Hopkinsville in 1906, the year of his first encounter with the sleeping subject. Since Cayce was pretty much unknown in those days, it is probable that Sadler first encountered him during a demonstration of Cayce's psychic powers for a Chautauqua meeting in the autumn of 1906.

Some confusion of beginning dates for the Urantia phenomenon has arisen since Sadler gave both 1906 and 1911 as beginning dates. However, when the reader understands that Sadler *encountered* the sleeping subject in 1906, but did not begin to actively study him until 1911, the mystery of two beginning dates vanishes. When Sadler first witnessed him, the sleeping subject was in an unconscious state and had no idea that Sadler was even there. They did not actually become *involved* with each other until Sadler was brought into contact with it in 1911 and began studying the sleeping subject at his institute.

Ecce Quam Bonum
"Behold How Good"[96]

The Bowling Green E.Q.B. Literary Club was formed in January of 1903. In June of that year, Dr.'s John Blackburn, James Blackburn and Hugh Beazley began to investigate Cayce. By 1906 Dr.'s Fred Reardon, Fred Cartwright, and

---

[96] E.Q.B stands for Ecce Quam Bonum, a Latin phrase which means "Behold how good".

George Meredith, had also become involved in the investigation. All of these doctors, except Dr. Meredith, were members of the E.Q.B.

That autumn, Cayce was invited to give a demonstration of his psychic ability at a meeting.

Three Different Accounts of the 1906 Meeting

The Cayce biographers record this public gathering as a literary club meeting. Here is what Thomas Sugrue wrote:

> In the autumn of 1906 the E.Q.B. Literary Club chose hypnosis for the subject of one of its monthly dinner meetings. By way of demonstration, Edgar was invited to give a reading. Most of the local doctors were to be at the dinner, and many physicians from surrounding localities. At the meeting Edgar went to sleep on the couch that was brought in and placed before the dais. He was given the name and address of a college student who was ill in a dormitory just outside the city. The boy was a patient of one of the doctors present.
>
> "Yes, we have the body," he said. "He is recovering from an attack of typhoid fever. The pulse is 96, the temperature is 101.4."
>
> The doctor in charge of the patient said the diagnosis was correct. A committee of three was dispatched to check on the temperature and pulse. While they were gone an argument arose as to what state of consciousness or unconsciousness Edgar was in.
>
> Some said hypnosis, some said trance, some said a dream state. The doctors who were witnessing their first reading wanted to find out. Over Blackburn's violent protests one of them stuck a needle in Edgar's arms, hands, and feet. There was no response. [97]

---

[97] Sugrue, 137.

Joseph Millard, in his book *Edgar Cayce: Mystery Man of Miracles*, describes it this way:

> There was to be a meeting that fall with a large number of local and out-of-town doctors attending ... He [Edgar Cayce] lay down on a couch in front of the crowd and gave a demonstration reading on a patient under treatment of one of the physicians ... [They] began to pinch and poke at Edgar, lifting his eyelids to peer into his eyes and prying open his mouth.
>
> "He can't feel a thing," one [doctor] said. "Completely anaesthetized, and I'll prove it."
>
> Before [John] Blackburn could elbow his way back, his angry protests unheeded, they had jabbed Edgar with pins, rammed a hat pin completely through his cheek and pried under one fingernail with a knife blade. There was neither nervous reaction nor blood.[98]

Jess Stearn, another author, describes the same event this way:

> The Hopkinsville Literary Club, in a gala opening of the new social season, had chosen hypnotism as the subject of a public demonstration. There were perhaps three hundred persons at the benefit affair. To the delight of the spectators, Cayce stretched out on a couch placed on the stage [and gave a reading]. The doctors turned back to the slumbering figure. Two or three got to wrangling over Cayce's state of consciousness, disagreeing whether it was a hypnotic trance or a dream state, or whether he was faking completely.
>
> Huddled in conference before the couch, they effectively screened the prostrate Cayce from the throng. As [Al] Layne looked on horrified, one of the doctors drew a long surgical needle from a black leather bag and deliberately thrust the needle into the sleeping man's arm. There was

---

[98] Millard, 95.

no visible reaction. He then stuck the needle into Cayce's hands. Still there was no response. "Well, he ought to feel this." The doctor scowled, sticking the needle sharply into the soles of Cayce's feet. There was not the slightest response.[99]

The Private E.Q.B. Files

Pursuing the reference of the E.Q.B. Literary Club, I contacted Dr. Keith Coverdale in Bowling Green, Kentucky, in June of 1995. He had been a club member for 25 years. I asked him if Cayce had ever given a demonstration for the E.Q.B. I told him that according to my information, Cayce gave a demonstration in 1906 for the club, and explained that I was attempting to verify the information. He said he would check with Charles R. Bryant, who was the club secretary. I also spoke with Dr. Jesse Funk, the nephew of Dr. John Blackburn. Dr. Funk said that his uncle told him many strange stories about Cayce, which he did not believe. Dr. Funk also said that as far as he knew, records for the E.Q.B. were kept back to it's very beginning in 1903. Six months later, in December 1995, I spoke with Dr. Coverdale again. He said he and Charles Bryant had gone through the club minutes and there were no references to Cayce. This indicated that Cayce had never been present at any of the E.Q.B. meetings.

The Size of the E.Q.B. Meetings

By comparing the statements of the three different authors, what can be learned about the event? In two of the accounts, John Blackburn was named as being at the meeting. He was a

---

[99] Stearn, 28-34.

charter member of the E.Q.B. Literary Club in Bowling Green. For three years, he and other local doctors who were members of the E.Q.B., had been investigating Cayce. Since Blackburn invited Cayce to give the demonstration, and other members of the E.Q.B were in attendance, Sugrue may have assumed that the meeting was that of the E.Q.B. Club.

But, the E.Q.B. was a private group of twelve men who met alternately in each other's residences, or at other pre-designated places for dinner. According to the club's by-laws, they never allowed anyone but members in attendance at their dinner meetings.

Sugrue wrote that the couch that Cayce laid down upon was placed before a dais. A dais is an elevated platform, in a large room or hall, such as would be in a Chautauqua meeting.

Stearn informs us that it was a public meeting at which Cayce gave his demonstration. He said the couch was placed on a stage and there were approximately 300 people present. These comments suggest the meeting was not a meeting of the small, private E.Q.B. meetings.

My conclusion is that the meeting was a Chautauqua gathering and some of the E.Q.B. members who were investigating Cayce at that time, attended the meeting. Further support for this theory is the large size of the meeting, which would be consistent with the potential of an entertaining and popular Chautauqua event.

William Randolph Hearst

5. The Hearsts, the Fields, and the Kelloggs

Cayce started to gain national publicity in newspapers across the country in late 1910. When Hearst learned of Cayce, he sent Roswell Field to interview him in February of 1911. Roswell was the younger brother of the famous newspaperman and author Eugene Field. Eugene was recently deceased, but very well-known and so popular that a society was formed in his honor, dubbed the Eugene Field Society of Chicago, and Dr. Sadler was a member. Sadler's in-laws provided many fortuitous crosscurrents for the development of his career and reputation. Sadler's book *The Mind at Mischief* was published by one of Hearst's publishing companies.

After Roswell returned to Chicago and turned in his findings to Hearst, a headline story appeared on the front page of the Chicago *Examiner*. This is what the article was about:

PSYCHIST DIAGNOSES AND CURES PATIENTS
IGNORANT OF MEDICINE, TURNS HEALER IN TRANCE
Kentuckian New Puzzle for Physicians
Admits he can remember nothing that occurs in hypnotic sleep

Hearst wanted more information about Cayce. So, after the article appeared in the Chicago *Examiner*, Mr. Hearst invited Cayce to Chicago on an all-expense paid visit. While Cayce was in Chicago he spent ten days giving readings.[100]

As you will see, Roswell Field's family connections included Dr. Sadler and his wife, Lena Kellogg, which made the Sadlers likely candidates to be called in to study Cayce.

Roswell Field's great grandmother was Ester Smith Kellogg and Lena's father was Moses Smith Kellogg. Roswell's

---

[100] Sugrue, 164.

grandfather was Charles Kellogg Field and his grandmother was Julia Ann Kellogg.

The Field family and the Kellogg family had genealogical history dating back many generations. Dr. Sadler was closely associated with John Harvey Kellogg of Battle Creek, Michigan, for many years, and married his niece.

This made Roswell Field (who was investigating Cayce on Hearst's behalf) a relative of the Sadler's. They were the only family members of the Fields and Kelloggs who happened to be the owners and founders of an institute, which was created specifically to study the subconscious mind, including the study of psychics and mediums. Not only that, but their Institute was located in Chicago, as were the offices of the Chicago *Examiner* newspaper.

Here's what Cayce had to say about the Chicago Institute: "I've always enjoyed my little visits to the Institute in Chicago. I don't believe I've ever been there that I haven't spent some time in the Institute. Something has always seemed to draw me there. Even on my first visit many, many years ago, when I went there as the guest of Mr. Hearst's paper, I spent most of my time in the Institute." [101]

Dr. Sadler admitted that he used hypnosis on the sleeping subject.[102] Perhaps this is why Cayce stated that *something always seemed to draw him back* to the Institute whenever he was in Chicago. One wonders if he may have received a post-hypnotic suggestion.

_____

[101] *The Complete Edgar Cayce Readings*, Document #35356, 2155-004 Reports (letter   written by Cayce - 11/29/32).
[102] Sadler, *Mind at Mischief*, 383.

After leaving Chicago and returning to Hopkinsville on March 24, 1911, the very next reading that Cayce gave recommended health food products from Battle Creek.[103] This was a reference to yogurt that was produced by the Kellogg Sanitarium, where the Sadlers had both been employed. Up until this time, the readings had never mentioned Kellogg's health food products. But thereafter, the readings mentioned Dr. John Harvey Kellogg, Kellogg's Sanitarium, Kellogg's health food products, and treatments used by Dr. Kellogg. The readings also made one mention of the Chicago Institution of Research.

Cayce had the habit of reading the minds of others that were in close proximity to him during readings. After visiting the Institute in Chicago, his subconscious mind had gathered information about Kellogg products from somewhere. I consider it likely that Cayce had been at Dr. Sadler's Institute in 1911.

However nowhere in the material that I have studied, have I found a statement that clearly identified Dr. Sadler's Institute as the Institute that Cayce visited. But where else could Cayce have been giving readings in 1911, in Chicago, at an institute, while in the proximity of persons whose subconscious minds contained information about Kellogg's health food products?

-----

[103] *The Complete Edgar Cayce Readings*, Document #46082, 3893-001 Text, (3/24/11).

Harry J. Loose

6. Harry Loose and Harold Sherman

Initially, my thinking was to investigate anyone that was involved with Sadler to see if he or she was involved with Cayce. It was amazing where some of these queries led. I had read G. Vonne Meussling's doctoral thesis on the life of Dr. Sadler as Chautauqua's medic orator. I discovered that John Harvey Kellogg had attempted to get Sadler interested in Jane Addams' work with Hull House, an organization that helped Chicago's underprivileged. A police officer named Harry Loose was working there. Although Sadler wasn't interested in getting involved with Hull House,[104] he did get involved with Loose.

Loose's career in police work began in 1901 with the Illinois State Police in Springfield, Indiana. He moved to Chicago where he became a Police Officer in 1906.

Sadler's involvement with Chautauqua appears to have appealed to Loose. The doctor had developed some friends during his career as a Chautauqua lecturer, and in February of 1917, he wrote a letter of recommendation for Loose to the President of the International Lyceum Bureau. Thereafter, Loose became a speaker for Chautauqua and traveled about giving talks on his experience as a Police Officer.

In 1921, one of Loose's Chautauqua speaking engagements was in Marion, Indiana. A reporter who worked for the Marion *Chronicle* newspaper, Harold Morrow Sherman, was assigned to cover the event. Afterwards, they met back at Loose's hotel to talk further and discovered a mutual interest in psychic phenomena. That night Sherman witnessed Loose telepathically communicating with his wife, as he did every night at midnight while traveling away from home. Sherman was deeply impressed by what he saw and heard during that visit. The two men soon lost track of each other however, though Sherman attempted unsuccessfully to locate Loose for many years.

---

[104] Meussling, 29.

In 1937 Sherman conducted experiments in long-distance telepathy with Sir Hubert Wilkins. Wilkins had been involved with Dr. Sadler and the Urantia revelation for years by this time. (see page 105 for details)

According to Dr. Sadler, the sleeping subject demonstrated telepathic ability, which mirrored that exhibited by Cayce. (See page 99, h.)

In the early years of the twentieth century, telepathic communication was referred to as 'thought transference' and later became known as mental telepathy. In a reading given in 1923 Cayce explained that the thoughts of one person could affect another person, depending upon the development of the individual to whom the thought was directed. He explained that thought transference was now being developed in individuals.[105] In 1925, he again explained the evolution of thought transference as the process of focusing thoughts to one point, which caused the condition to become accentuated by the force of the thought manifested, which then became real. He explained that thought transmission, or transference, occurred when both persons were in the same subconscious condition.[106]

After the completion of the telepathic experiments, Sherman and Wilkins co-authored *Thoughts Through Space*, a book giving an account of their telepathic experiences. Wilkins had flown across the Arctic in search of a missing Russian aircraft and its crew. During the search, he sent telepathic messages to Sherman in New York. Afterwards, Sherman had this to say:

> With the finish of these experiments and with time to study and evaluate them, it became clear to me that I had,

---

[105] *The Complete Edgar Cayce Readings*, Document 45026, 3744-002, Text, (10/9/23).
[106] *The Complete Edgar Cayce Readings*, Document 20902, 0900-023, Text, (1/18/25).

in my ways, been able to receive specific and detailed impressions of events from Wilkins' mind, comparable to the type of communication that Harry Loose and his wife had apparently demonstrated years before. I had never doubted the validity of what I had witnessed that night in the Marion Hotel, and my memory of it had given me the faith that if I persisted, I would hopefully, one day, acquire the ability to duplicate what the Looses had done.

Thinking of them so strongly renewed my desire to make contact with Harry again, and one day, as if in response to this desire, an amazing thing happened. The chances for this occurrence were literally 10,000 to 1, for Wilkins and I received some 10,000 letters from people all over the world, following publication of a feature article in the March 1939 issue of *Cosmopolitan* magazine, telling about the success of our long-distance telepathic adventure.

Harold Sherman requested readings from Edgar Cayce on 11/2/38, 12/23/38, 1/19/39, and 2/9/39. He was also involved with Hugh Lynn Cayce on the production of a radio program called Mysteries of the Mind, during this same time period. Sherman's involvement with the Cayces occurred during his involvement with Wilkins! Since Wilkins' and Sherman's experiments centered around the paranormal, there can be little doubt that Sherman and Wilkins discussed the phenomenon associated with Edgar Cayce.

We divided the mail between us and set out to try to reply to all the interested correspondents, a task which took some months.

As I was writing Walter D. Germain, head of the Crime Prevention Department, Saginaw Police Force, Saginaw Michigan, I suddenly had the feeling that he might know the whereabouts of Harry J. Loose; so - acting on impulse - I added a postscript: Would you happen to know the present address of Harry J. Loose, former Chicago policeman and detective in charge of Hull House? If so, I would greatly appreciate your sending it to me.

An immediate reply came from Harry, indicative in every way of the unusual nature and character of the man as I had remembered and been inspired by him. The first of many treasured communications we were to receive from February 4, 1941, until the time of his passing, November 21, 1943.[107]

By 1941, Sherman had become an accomplished author, and Warner Brothers in Hollywood, California became interested in his screenplay, Mark Twain. Harold and Martha Sherman moved to California and lived a short distance from Harry Loose.

How did Warner Brothers become interested in Sherman's play? Once again our investigation led us to Cayce!

A surprising discovery showed that a reading by Cayce was ultimately responsible for Sherman getting involved with Warner Brothers and moving to California, where he learned of the Urantia project from Loose!

On January 2, 1939, a businessman in New York (referred to as Mr. [437] in the A.R.E. files) asked for a reading from Cayce. He was involved with the cinema industry and was asking advice about what motion picture he should produce. The readings recommended using the play written by Harold Sherman on the life of Mark Twain, and also suggested using Warner Brothers and Sam Goldwyn of Los Angeles![108] This reading resulted in Sherman's interaction with Loose, Dr. Sadler, and the Forum!

Sherman stated:

> At different times during our visits together, Harry re-ferred to the great book-to-be, known as The Great Reve-lation Book [The Book of Urantia] which he hoped we

---

[107] Harold Sherman, *How to Know What to Believe* (Greenwich: Fawcett, 1976) 36-37.

[108] *The Complete Edgar Cayce Readings*, Document 12994, 0437-010 Text, (1/2/39).

would one day, be able to read in manuscript form; and he hoped that we would have the opportunity to confer with the doctor in charge of this extraordinary revelation, as well as to get acquainted with members of the Forum studying the papers in residence in the city of Chicago. We began to make plans to do just that.[109]

In July of 1941 Mr. & Mrs. Sherman stopped in Chicago to meet Dr. Sadler and were accepted as Forum members. It was perhaps because of Sherman's profession as a writer, the recent Mark Twain work, and the reputation that had come to him through the experiment in long-distance telepathy with Wilkins, that he and Mrs. Sherman were so quickly accepted by Sadler into the Forum. On the evening of August 20, 1942, Sadler was in a talkative mood and told Harold and Martha about his first encounter with the sleeping subject about 35 years previously. He revealed the following details alluding to the identity of the sleeping subject:

(a.)   the man was married
(b.)   he was a businessman
(c.)   he was involved in some way with the stock market
(d.)   the man's wife had fear as a result of the phenomenon
(e.)   the phenomenon was different than other so-called trance states of other mediums
(f.)   the man's body experienced jumps and starts
(g.)   respiration was sometimes markedly interfered with,[110] breathing was sometimes labored[111]
(h.)   the man could read Sadler's thoughts and answered questions before they were asked[112]
(i.)   the man was approaching middle age

---

[109] Sherman, 57
[110] Sadler, *Mind at Mischief*, 383.
[111] Sherman, 63.
[112] Sherman, 65.

(j.)   the doctor tried to arouse him by sticking pins in him, but failed[113]

The foregoing points that Sadler covered during that conversation, match precisely with Edgar Cayce's life about 35 years previously, in the autumn of 1906. Compare the following list of items from Cayce's life to that of Sadler's remarks about the sleeping subject.

(a.)   Cayce was married in 1903 to Gertrude Evans.[114]
(b.)   Cayce was a businessman who operated his own photography business.[115]
(c.)   Cayce invented a Board of Trade game he called "Pit"[116] and gave readings on the stock market, speaking the trade jargon of stockbrokers.
(d.)   Gertrude was experiencing some fear in 1906, resulting from the psychic phenomenon exhibited by Cayce.[117]
(e.)   Cayce did not operate as a medium in the usual sense of that word.[118]
(f.)   Cayce's body experienced jerking and twitching movements.[119]

---

[113] Sherman, 61-63.
[114] Sugrue, 121.
[115] Sugrue, 129, 130.
[116] Sugrue, 119.
       Leary, 32.
[117] Sugrue, 139.
[118] Agee, 40.
       Hugh Lynn Cayce, *Venture Inward*, 104.
       Furst, 302.
       The Complete Edgar Cayce Readings, Document 4028, 0254-063
       Reports, (4/26/32).
[119] Agee, 48.

(g.)   There were times when the passing hours were marked by Cayce's flagging respiration.[120]

(h.)   The sleeping Cayce answered questions before they could be asked.[121]

(i.)   Cayce was 29 in 1906 -- approaching middle age, life expectancy in the mortality tables at that time was 48.5 years for a white adult male.[122]

(j.)   *One doctor* suck pins into Cayce in an attempt to awaken him, but failed.[123]

For more detail about the timing of events in the lives of Cayce and Sadler, see Appendix D: Cayce-Urantia Timeline.

---

[120] Bro, *Edgar Cayce on Religion and Psychic Experience*, 21.

[121] Bro, *Edgar Cayce on Religion and Psychic Experience*, 28.

[122] Meussling, 3.

[123] Joseph Millard, *Edgar Cayce: Mystery Man of Miracles* (Greenwich, Conn.: Fawcett, 1967) 95.

  Jess Stearn, *A Prophet in His Own Country* (New York: Morrow, 1974) 28-34.

  Sugrue, 137.

Harold Sherman

7. Sherman and Cayce

As previously revealed, Sherman interacted with Hugh Lynn Cayce in producing a radio program about stories of psychic phenomenon. This led to Sherman becoming involved with Edgar Cayce.

Many documents included in *The Complete Edgar Cayce Readings* on CD-ROM make reference to Sherman. Several of these documents reveal that Sherman thought highly of Cayce, and received readings for himself.[124]

According to Sherman in his *book How to Know What to Believe*, at one time he was being considered as Cayce's biographer, because Thomas Sugrue was very ill.[125] However, Sugrue recovered and Sherman did not write Cayce's biography.

The health reading that Cayce gave for Sherman recommended electrical therapy. The electrical treatment was administered incorrectly by a physician. Sherman blamed Cayce,[126] and became embittered toward him.

After Sherman's disassociation with Edgar Cayce, two years passed before Sherman met Dr. Sadler and became involved with the Urantia Papers.[127] This lapse of time combined with the secrecy in the Forum helps explain why Sherman did not associate Cayce as being Sadler's sleeping subject.

---

[124] *The Complete Edgar Cayce Readings*, Document numbers: 4186, 4185, 4181, 12994, 13008, 25874, 25894, 25898, 25902, 31669, 31670, 31671, 31672, 31673, 31674, 31675, 31676, 31677, 31678, 31679, 31680, 31681, 31682, 31683, 31684, 32226, 33229, 33231, 33232, 44372.

[125] Sherman, 111-12, 116-17.

[126] Sherman, 114-16.

[127] Sherman, Chap. 7.

Sir Hubert Wilkins

8. Sherman and Wilkins

After being admitted to the Forum as a new member in 1941, Harold Sherman contacted Sir Hubert Wilkins,[128] and explained the Chicago revelation.   However, author John Grierson revealed in his biography of Wilkins, that in correspondence to his secretary Winston Ross, Wilkins stated that he had already been involved with the Urantia project for over 20 years by 1955, and was also a member of the later Urantia Foundation.[129]

In 1941, Sherman was not aware that Wilkins had already been involved with Dr. Sadler for many years and apparently Wilkins did not divulge this information to Sherman, because Sherman always assumed responsibility for Wilkins' involvement with Urantia.

It was characteristic of Wilkins to be very tight-lipped, which fact Grierson revealed about Wilkins' covert nature. Grierson disclosed that Wilkins was even secretive toward his wife.

Dr. Sadler's decision to include Sherman in his inner circle turned out to be a mistake. Friction developed within the group due to personality clashes between Dr. Sadler and Mr. Sherman. Eventually Mr. and Mrs. Sherman discontinued their association with Dr. Sadler and left Chicago in 1947, but continued to maintain contact with Wilkins.

In a letter to Sir Hubert Wilkins on December 16, 1950 Sherman wrote, "We still feel that parts of this book have been humanly tampered with."[130] Again on February 10, 1957 he

---

[128] See p. 100 for more information on the association of Wilkins and Sherman.

[129] Wilkins Archives, Byrd Polar Research Center, Ohio State University.

[130] Wilkins Archives, box 12, folder 42 -- letter from Sherman to Wilkins dated 12/16/1950.

stated, "I know that some of the material did not come from the original source."[131]

---

[131] Wilkins Archives, box 13, folder 5 -- letter from Sherman to Wilkins dated 2/10/1957.

9. Sir Hubert Wilkins - The Missing Link

In 1924 George Hubert Wilkins arrived in America. Wilkins planned to make an unprecedented attempt at becoming the first man to explore the Arctic in an airplane. He had accumulated fifteen thousand dollars of funding before his arrival in America. He approached the North American Newspaper Alliance, which was willing to invest twenty-five thousand dollars for rights to the story.[132] Upon completion of this flight, Wilkins traveled from the Arctic to London where he was knighted as Sir Hubert Wilkins. (Wilkins had a brother named George, who had died in infancy, so when he was knighted, he chose to use his middle name, Hubert.)

Before he reached London, he began planning to fly over Antarctica.[133]

In 1927 Wilkins came back to America to seek support for his new attempt at Antarctic exploration and met with William Randolph Hearst, owner of the Hearst newspapers. Wilkins sold Hearst the exclusive rights to publish the story.

Over the years, Wilkins had developed a keen interest in psychic phenomena, as did Hearst from his investigation of Cayce. It is uncertain how Wilkins was introduced to Sadler, but he became involved with Sadler and the Urantia Papers at least two decades before the publication of *The Urantia Book*.[134] Dr. Sadler admitted having consultation with Wilkins during the early years of the Urantia phenomenon.[135]

When Wilkins flew over the Antarctic in 1928, during one particular flight he made two discoveries. One he named Hearst Land, in honor of Mr. Hearst for funding the expedition. The other he named Casey Channel. I've often wondered why

---

[132] Grierson, 100.
[133] Grierson, 120-21.
[134] Grierson, 203.
[135] Kulieke, 4.

Wilkins chose these particular two names for his discoveries that were in such close proximity to each other. Wilkins never made it clear.

In an interview for the Hearst Newspapers in 1911, Cayce told Roswell Field that the Cayces came from France many years ago, and one of his grandfathers married an Irish girl, thus showing the possible confusion of Cayce for Casey, names that were pronounced exactly alike.[136]

Could it be that Wilkins named Casey Channel after Edgar Cayce?

STATEMENT OF POLICY COVERING
GEOGRAPHICAL NAMES IN ANTARCTICA
(dated July 13, 1946)

These policies are for the guidance of the Board in deciding cases and for the guidance of explorers and others in proposing names for natural features in Antarctica.

The problem of geographic nomenclature is different for Antarctica than for any other part of the world. It has no permanent settlements. Even in the explored portions of the continent many of the features are unnamed, and still others have never been seen by man. Antarctica has been visited and explored by the nationals of many nations, who, by their heroic efforts to broaden man's knowledge of this land of ice and snow, have fully demonstrated the international nature of world science. Names, therefore, will be considered without reference to the nationality of the person honored.

Under the policy here set forth, decisions on Antarctic names will be based on priority of application, appropriateness, and the extent to which usage has become established. The grouping of natural features into three orders of magnitude, with corresponding categories of persons according to the type of contribution which they have

---

[136] A. Robert Smith, *The Lost Memoirs of Edgar Cayce*, 100.

made, is intended to provide the greatest possible objectivity in determining the appropriateness of a name. It does not, however, exclude the use of other than personal names when appropriate. Non personal names are discussed under a separate heading.

Inappropriate Names

Names in the following categories will not be considered, unless otherwise appropriate according to the principles stated herein, or unless such names are widely and firmly established as of the date of approval of these principals.

1. Names suggested because of relationship or friendship
2. Names of contributors of funds

These policies were not in effect until after Wilkins made his Antarctic explorations. Following this lead (the naming of the Antarctic discoveries) I contacted the National Geographic Society in Australia. They referred me to the Sir Hubert Wilkins Foundation, which was an organization founded to preserve the Wilkins estate as a historic landmark. The Foundation could provide no information concerning the naming of either of Wilkins' discoveries.

However, The National Geographic Society of Australia did inform me that Wilkins' great niece lived in Australia and gave me her mailing address. I wrote to her to see if she could provide any insight into my investigation. Weeks went by and one day I received a reply, saying that she maintained a collection of memorabilia from her great uncle's life, but had no information that could be of help concerning my investigation. This ended the possibility of receiving direct information from Australia, but another development opened a new door.

While reading the biography written by John Grierson about Wilkins, I was surprised to discover that he named Wilkins as a

contributor to *The Urantia Book*![137]   He admitted he did not
know the extent of Wilkins contribution. Another of Wilkins'
biographers, Lowell Thomas, also provided a clue, which
connected Wilkins with *The Urantia Book*. Both biographers
included a prayer written by Wilkins. (See p. 143-144)

Further searching led to the discovery of the Admiral Perry
Byrd Polar Research Institute archives, which contained the
Wilkins archives![138]   These were located at the University of
Ohio. The archives contained abundant information about Wil-
kins and also contained some of his correspondence with
Sherman. There was also a letter from Bill Sadler, Jr., along
with a letter and a Christmas card from Dr. William S. Sadler.
One file folder contained a membership card designating Wil-
kins' membership with the International Lyceum Association.
Other letters and miscellaneous information connected Wilkins
with Hearst. One letter dated May 22, 1936 from Hearst to
Wilkins stated:

> Dear Hubert:
>   I appreciate very highly the honor of having Hearst Land
> so named, and thank you for your kindness in sending me
> the photographs of the territory.[139]

Also, there was a record of Wilkins staying at the Monticello
Hotel, in Norfolk, Virginia. Cayce lived in Norfolk during a
portion of his life.[140]

---

[137] Grierson, bibliography, 8.

[138] Once Wilkins' connection to *The Urantia Book* was established, we looked
for anything that he may have authored, and discovered the archived
material that way.

[139] Wilkins Archives, box 12, folder 26 – letter from William Randolph Hearst
dated 5/22/36.

[140] Wilkins Archives, box 2, folder 3 – letter on hotel stationary.

Additional records showed Wilkins staying in Chicago at the Diversey Arms Hotel, one block from Sadler's Institute and residence, which were located on the same street.[141]

Other letters in the archives sometimes referred to the group in Chicago and the manuscript they studied.[142]   But, in my opinion the most noteworthy item discovered was a letter written by Wilkins to his personal Secretary Winston Ross. It was dated November 1, 1955, which was one month after the publication of *The Urantia Book*! Here is a portion of the letter:

> Dear Winston,
> For many years I have been associated with a group in Chicago which has been interested in publishing some Papers of material revealed to us by visitors from outer universes. At last we have been able to print and privately distribute the Book and I would like for you to have a copy.
> At present we are not telling many of the recipients of the manner in which the information was received but I can tell you for your own information that the texts of the papers were spoken by the revelators through a man in his sleep and who *to this day has no idea that he was the medium.* [emphasis mine]

At last it became clear that the sleeping subject was never told about the Urantia information that came through him. Now I knew my theory regarding this issue had been correct.

> Learning that this man was "talking in his sleep" it was arranged to have a stenographer record the statements and soon it was possible for those concerned not only to listen and record, but to also talk with the revelators as you and I might talk.

---

[141] Wilkins Archives, box 2, folder 3 – letter on hotel stationary.
[142] Wilkins Archives, box 12, folder 43 – letter to Wilkins dated 9/13/51.

The mass of information of the Book is at first bewildering. To most of us it came piece by piece and was not
overwhelming.

How much of it you and your mother might accept of the
information I do not know, but if you can accept it the
information as to the possibilities of survival after death
and the experiences thereafter, as mentioned in the paper
Morontia Life and elsewhere is most inspiring, and com-
forting.

Best regards,
Hubert

10. The Two Magicians

Howard Thurston

Sadler believed that all manifestations associated with psychics and mediums were either fraudulent or tricks of the subconscious mind.

He had the sleeping subject under observation at the Chicago Institute of Research and Diagnosis where he submitted him to hypnotism to explore his subconscious. [143] Sadler had trouble getting him under, but when he finally did so, he found no consciousness whatsoever of the subjects discussed by these purported beings, which Sadler had, by this time, started to record.

Hypnotists who attempted to hypnotize Cayce experienced trouble getting him under as well. [144]

Sadler said, "I now felt that I needed help in solving the causes behind this mysterious phenomenon, and I called in other doctors and scientists, friends of mine, as well as Houdini and Thurston. They were equally unable to furnish any explanation."[145]

Howard Thurston was a well-known magician and illusionist in the early part of the century. He spent some of his time investigating and exposing fraudulent mediums. The American public's attention was turned toward psychic phenomenon and mediumistic events during that time in history. Newspapers were continually publishing stories about psychics and mediums. Some of the well-known magicians of those times advertised themselves as 'psychic investigators,' to enhance

---

[143] Sadler, *Mind at Mischief*, 383.
[144] Sugrue, 104.
    Furst, 338.
[145] Sherman, 64.

publicity and take advantage of the public's interest in the occult.

Howard Thurston & Harry Houdini

One day in 1923, the famous magician Howard Thurston had lunch with Dr. Sadler.[146] Dr. Sadler thought that Mr. Thurston was the greatest magician on stage in those days. Thurston explained that he believed that all psychic demonstrations performed as a commercial proposition for money were fraudulent.

Cayce neither performed commercially nor asked for money, and wanted only to use his psychic ability for the betterment of mankind.[147]

Harry Houdini

Houdini was an author as well as a world famous magician. His articles appeared in many magazines. He also wrote articles for hundreds of newspapers, among them, Hearst's.[148]

Beginning in 1921, the exposure of fraud in mediumistic practice absorbed Houdini more and more. Thereafter, he gave 24 lectures in February 1924 in cities in the Middle West and South.[149] Houdini may have been a member of the International Lyceum Association, but I have not investigated that subject.

When Houdini got back from his lecture tour in the spring of 1924, he began building himself as an expert in the field of psychic investigation.[150] That same year he had written his latest book, *Houdini: A Magician Among the Spirits*, in which he stated:

> Mine has not been an investigation of a few days or weeks or months but one that has extended over thirty years and in that thirty years I have not found one incident that savored of the genuine. If there had been any real

---

[146] Sadler, *The Truth About Spiritualism*, 119.
[147] Sugrue, 6.
[148] Milbourne Christopher, *Houdini: A Pictorial Life* (New York: Crowell, c1976) 113.
[149] Kellock, Harold. *Houdini: His Life Story*, 326.
[150] Gresham, William L. *Houdini: The Man Who Walked Through Walls*, 240.

unalloyed demonstration to work on, one that did not reek
of fraud, one that could not be reproduced by earthly
powers, then there would be something for a foundation,
but up to the present time everything that I have investigated has been the result of deluded brains or those which
were too actively and intensely willing to believe.[151]

It can be deduced that Houdini had not met the sleeping
subject at this point in his life, nor had he observed the contact
phenomena associated with the Urantia Papers. This is clear,
because Sadler stated that after calling him in on the matter,
Houdini could not explain the phenomenon. Up to this time,
Houdini had been able to explain and reproduce every performance of so-called spiritualist phenomena that he had ever
encountered.

In the latter portion of 1925, Houdini performed in Chicago
for eight weeks.[152] He had developed a profound interest in
psychic research due to the death of his mother, and became
obsessed with learning about the life hereafter. In the process
of his search for legitimate spiritual contact, Houdini had ex-
posed many fraudulent mediums. While he was in Chicago, he
and his staff investigated more than forty mediums.[153]

Several of Dr. Sadler's Forum members stated that Houdini
was involved with Sadler and the case of the sleeping subject.[154]
Considering that Houdini had never encountered any genuine
psychic phenomena that he could not explain or reproduce by
1924, and since he died in October of 1926, he may have
witnessed Sadler's sleeping subject in 1925.

---

[151] Harry Houdini, *Houdini: A Magician among the Spirits* (New York: Arno, 1972).
[152] Christopher, Milbourne. *Houdini: Untold Story* (New York: Crowell, 1969) 166-172.
[153] Christopher, *Houdini: Untold Story*, 225.
[154] Telephone conversation, 1/23/96 between the author and Mark Kulieke. Kulieke, 6.

Here is a letter written by Cayce in February 1933, in which he stated:

> I knew Mr. Houdini personally during his lifetime. I had the privilege of seeing him do some of his tricks, as he called them, that certainly took on the air of something far beyond just tricks. As he expressed it himself, he was very much afraid to allow himself to admit that something outside of him had controlled his activities. Also I had the privilege of making an experiment or demonstration for him, with several very well known medical men present and some students of psychic phenomena. He had made the statement that he had never seen anything done by a medium or one in a trance that he couldn't duplicate. After seeing the demonstration, and the patient which the doctors later examined and found to be true to that given, he expressed the opinion that it far exceeded anything he had ever seen, and that it was, of course, entirely out of the class of mediumistic control, but as to what was the source he wouldn't like to say-because he didn't know.[155]

Houdini had not witnessed Cayce's demonstration prior to 1924. But before his death in 1926, Houdini had met Dr. Sadler, witnessed a demonstration by the sleeping subject *and* had also witnessed a demonstration of the sleeping Cayce's ability. In both cases, he could offer no explanation and had never seen anything like it before. Could it be that the sleeping subject and Edgar Cayce were one and the same person? To me, it was looking more and more like Cayce was Sadler's sleeping subject.

---

[155] *The Complete Edgar Cayce Readings*, Document #13576, 0464-013 Reports, (1/17/33).

11. The Publications

In October of 1955 *The Urantia Book* was published.

On November 1, 1955, Sir Hubert Wilkins sent a letter to his personal secretary, Winston Ross, accompanied by a copy of the newly published *Urantia Book*.

In November of 1955, the A.R.E. received a copy of *The Urantia Book* in the mail which was sent from the Urantia Brotherhood by Mrs. 3316, a Forum member for over 20 years.

Author John Grierson included part of Sir Wilkins' letter to Mr. Ross in his 1959 biography of Wilkins' life, *Sir Hubert Wilkins: Enigma of Exploration*

Sir Wilkins passed away in 1958, during the time author Lowell Thomas was writing his 1960 biography. Thomas had spent a considerable amount of time with Sir Wilkins, Lady Wilkins and Winston Ross, and had been granted access to personal letters and documents.

In 1964, *Venture Inward*, by Hugh Lynn Cayce, included *The Urantia Book* in a section titled: "Dangerous Doorways to the Unconscious." Hugh Lynn describes it as a "very complicated tome which has appeared, presenting new lists of heavenly beings previously not known to man."[156] Ironically, in the same book he states, "One should take time to read a book or two which critically appraise the whole field of psychic research," and then recommends "William S. Sadler, MD, *The Mind at Mischief*."[157] It appears that Hugh Lynn was not aware that Dr. Sadler was the primary person involved with *The*

---

[156] Cayce, *Venture Inward*, 127.
[157] Cayce, *Venture Inward*, 179.

Urantia Book, nor was he aware that in the Appendix of *The Mind at Mischief*, Dr. Sadler was referring to the person through whom the Urantia Papers were obtained. Also interesting is the fact that *Venture Inward* is the only book which mentions so many characters in this story: Edgar Cayce, *The Urantia Book*, the Urantia Foundation, Dr. William S. Sadler, *The Mind at Mischief*, Harold Sherman, and Sir Hubert Wilkins.

In 1974 Harold Sherman published his book titled *How to Know What to Believe*. In the fourth chapter he wrote of his involvement with Harry Loose. In the fifth chapter he wrote of his involvement with Dr. Sadler in Chicago, using fictitious names in some instances.

In 1991 Mark Kulieke, who is a son of members of Dr. Sadler's Forum, published *Birth of a Revelation*. In his book, Mark tells the story of *The Urantia Book* as various Forum members told it to him.

In 1995, Martin Gardner published a book which is critical of *The Urantia Book* and is titled *Urantia: The Great Cult Mystery*. It contains much previously unpublished information about persons and events involved with *The Urantia Book*.

And in 1996, the first draft of *Edgar Cayce and The Urantia Book* was created.

Part III: Stories Concerning
The Urantia Book

1. Remarks About Dr. Sadler's Papers

The History of the Urantia Movement is a group of papers, which are attributed to the authorship of Dr. Sadler, and appear in their entirety in Appendix A. The reader may notice that Sadler did not personally write these papers. Some of Sadler's statements are recorded in quotes, but it is obvious that someone else is telling this story. It was formulated many years after the events actually happened. These papers are undated, but were probably prepared in 1956, for a group of ministers from northern Indiana who had questions about the origin of the book. Later, in 1960, these papers were reproduced and published, but there were changes made to the original text of the document. Appendix A contains the complete original unpublished version.

One of the issues constantly encountered in this section is the question of how the Urantia papers were written. Were they written by the sleeping subject or were they written by a stenographer? And why is this relevant?

The majority of the Cayce material was recorded by someone else while he spoke during his sleep. There are only two indirect references to Cayce writing himself. Therefore, if most of the Urantia papers were actually hand written by the sleeping subject, he was not Cayce. However, the statements made by Dr. Sadler and his son Bill concerning this matter not only contradict each other, but at times contradict themselves.

My review of these papers is to present a picture of how they may have related to Cayce. The papers do not reveal the events in chronological order. Therefore, to the best of my ability, I have given the dates when these events occurred. The text of Dr. Sadler's papers is in bold type.

History of the Urantia Movement

Several members of this group who participated in the preliminary "contacts" which led up to the appearance of the Urantia Papers, had considerable experience in the investigation of psychic phenomena. This group early arrived at the conclusion that the phenomena connected with the personality, who was later associated with the Urantia Papers, was in no way similar to any other well-known type of psychic performance -- such as hypnotism, automatic writing, clairvoyance, trances, spirit mediumship, telepathy, or double personality.

Cayce always cautioned against the possible dangers to the individual when engaging in automatic writing. The readings advised, rather than using automatic writing or a medium, to turn to the voice within.[158]

It should be made clear that the antecedents of the Urantia Papers were in no way associated with so-called spiritualism -- with its seances and supposed communication with the spirits of departed human beings.

Cayce in no way wanted his spirituality confused with spiritualism.[159] Within the readings, he continually warned against communication with 'the dead' -- and all such occupations a automatic writing, séances, and Ouija boards."[160]

---

[158] Agee, 80.
[159] Leary, 86.
[160] Furst, 302.

Contact Activities Preceding the Urantia Papers

It would seem that, during these early years, our unseen friends were engaged in a thorough going testing of the contact personality, rehearsing the technique of communication, selecting the Contact Commissioners -- in fact, in a general way -- setting the stage for the subsequent initiation of the presentation of the "Urantia Papers."

During these early years we were introduced to many new and, to us, somewhat strange concepts of the universe of universes and as concerned man and his life on earth.

Among these numerous new ideas of cosmology and philosophy, the following mentioned topics in Dr. Sadler's papers are contained in the Cayce readings. These remarks, although expressed by Dr. Sadler in relation to the Urantia material, precisely describe Cayce's thinking and that of his associates concerning the phenomenon associated with the readings:

1. **New concept of a far-flung cosmos.**

2. **Millions of other inhabited worlds.**

3. **Introduction to scores of different and varied echelons of celestial personalities.**

4. **Confirmation of evolutionary origin of human-kind -- even of an evolutionary cosmos.**

5. **Intimation of multiple Creator Deities.**

6. **Tentative testing of our theologic concepts. Patient determination of how far we might possibly go in the direction of modifying our theologic beliefs and philosophical opinions.**

7. **Without realizing it, over a period of twenty years, our fundamental religious views and attitudes had been considerably changed.**

Our superhuman friends thus spent upward of two decades in extending our cosmic horizons, enlarging our theologic concepts, and expanding our over-all philosophy.

The information that the Forum received from the sleeping subject expanded their understanding. Similarly, the readings reveal the ever-broadening scope of Cayce's information.[161] But it wasn't just the information that was expanding. Cayce's ability to receive it was expanding as well.[162]

We never realized how our religious thinking had been expanded until the Papers began to arrive. As the Revelation progressed we came more fully to appreciate how we had been prepared for the vast alteration of our religious beliefs by these preliminary contacts extending over a period of twenty years of pre-education.

This pre-education period refers to the time from 1906, when Dr. Sadler first encountered the sleeping subject, until 1927, when the first Papers began to be given in response to questions formulated by the Forum.

------

[161] Agee, 61-62.
[162] Agee, 61-2.

During these early years, all of our observations and investigations utterly failed to reveal the psychic technique of reducing messages to writing.

Did Cayce ever write while he was unconscious? One reading refers to articles written by Cayce while in the trance state. [163] Another reading attempts to explain the psychic technique of how messages were reduced to writing (see p. 76 for details).

Cayce was also referred to as "the sleeping editor."[164]

---

[163] *The Complete Edgar Cayce Readings*, Document #3830, 0254-014 Text, (10/27/24).

[164] Agee, 67.

How the Urantia Papers Started

<u>1906</u> The contact process began in the autumn of this year.

<u>1927</u> **After about twenty years of contact experience, an alleged student-visitor, speaking through this sleeping subject during one of these nocturnal vigils...**

There are records of 238 readings given by Cayce at night. He probably gave more, but the exact number is unknown, since many readings are unaccounted for.

... in answer to one of our questions, said: "If you only knew what you are in contact with you would not ask such trivial questions. You would rather ask such questions as might elicit answers of supreme value to the human race."

<u>1962</u> Bill Sadler, Jr.'s version, "he said, if you knew what I knew you wouldn't ask these sort of half-baked questions. You would prepare some of the most deep, far-reaching and searching questions that could ever be asked."

<u>1927</u> The forces speaking through the sleeping Cayce challenged his listeners by saying: "Why is such communication so often of seemingly an unnecessary nature? Rather cultivate that of such communications, and receive the answer to that of the most profound that may be pro-pounded."[165]

---

[165] *The Complete Edgar Cayce Readings*, Document #57054, 5756-004 Text, #12, (3/17/27)

Approximately 20 years had elapsed from the beginning of the contact process (autumn of 1906) and the date of the above challenge (March 17, 1927) from the sleeping Cayce.

How the Forum Started

Dr. William S. Sadler, a member of this early group of observers and investigators, tells the following story regarding the origin of that group of interested individuals which later on became known as the "Forum." He says: "On my way to the University of Kansas to deliver some lectures on Gestalt psychology, I wrote a letter to my son, age 16, saying that I thought doctors should try to maintain some contact with their old patients. I suggested that he talk with his mother about the feasibility of inviting some of our old friends to meet with us on Sunday afternoons for an hour or two of informal discussion and social exchange.

<u>1923</u> "When I returned to Chicago one Sunday morning I found that my wife had invited a group of our old patients to meet at our house that afternoon at three o'clock. It was the plan to conduct these Sunday afternoon gatherings somewhat as follows: First have a talk on some health topic -- such as the treatment of common colds, the cause and cure of worry, and then, after a cup of tea, engage in informal discussions -- asking and answering questions.

Introduction of the Forum to the "Contacts"

<u>1923</u> **The doctor continues his narrative: "Presently, I was asked to give a series of talks on "Mental Hygiene," or "Psychic Phenomena." <u>At the beginning of my first talk,</u> I said: "With one or two exceptions, all of the psychic phenomena which I have investigated have turned out to be either conscious or unconscious frauds. Some were deliberate frauds -- others were those peculiar cases in which the performer was a victim of the deceptions of his own subconscious mind."** [emphasis mine]

"I had no more than said this, when one of the group spoke up, saying: "Doctor, if you have contacted something which you have been unable to solve -- it would be interesting -- tell us more about it."

<u>1923</u> MAY--Cayce was in Chicago giving readings and he always visited the Institute whenever he was in Chicago.

<u>1923</u> OCTOBER – **"I asked Dr. Lena to get some notes she had taken at a recent "contact" and read them to the group."**

<u>1962</u> Bill Sadler, Jr., "The Forum became intrigued with the shorthand notes that had been taken on things which this medium would talk about." (This is an example of some hand written papers containing information from the sleeping subject, *but the sleeping subject did not write them.*)

"It should be understood that up to this time there was no secrecy connected with this case. The Urantia Papers had not begun to appear.

"It was at about this time that this group meeting at our house on Sunday afternoons began to be called the "Forum."

"The group manifested such a great interest in this case <u>that I never did get around to giving any of the health talks</u> such as had been planned." [emphasis mine]

<u>1923</u> From day one, at the beginning of his first talk, Sadler told the Forum of the sleeping subject and shared information with them.

<u>1927</u> **"It was while these informal discussions were going on from week to week...**

These week-to-week discussions had been going on for four years before the challenge was given. Why did it take so long for the events to unfold? Perhaps because Cayce was only in Chicago periodically.

In *The Mind at Mischief*, Sadler said he observed the phenomenon periodically.

<u>1933</u> Cayce said he visited the Institute whenever he was in Chicago, beginning in 1911.

...that the challenge came to us suggesting that if we would ask more serious questions we might get information of value to all mankind."

<u>1927</u> A similar challenge came during a Cayce session (see p104).

The Forum Begins to Ask Questions

<u>1927</u> **"We told the Forum all about this and invited them to join us in the preparation of questions. We decided to start out with questions pertaining to the origin of the cosmos, Deity, creation, and such other subjects as were far beyond the present-day knowledge of all humankind.**

"The following Sunday several hundred questions were brought in. We sorted out these questions, discarding duplicates, and in a general way, classifying them. Shortly thereafter, the first Urantia Paper appeared in answer to these questions.

How did the first Paper appear? Here are some of the accounts:

<u>1962</u> Bill Sadler, Jr. said:

So the next Sunday when the Forum met, they came in on the deal. And I think -- I'm told -- that approximately 5,000 questions were assembled, many of them duplicates, some of them undoubtedly silly -- Who created God? How old is God? -- these are unanswerable questions. I haven't the foggiest notion of what was expected to transpire. Maybe they thought they were going over at sometime and read all these questions and take down the answers in shorthand. But what happened was this: One day the questions were gone, and where the papers had been kept was the first of the Urantia Papers, entitled 'The Universal Father'.

<u>1942</u> During a private interview in August of 1942, with Harold and Martha Sherman, Dr. Sadler is quoted as saying:

The following Sunday the group arrived with over four thousand questions! Lena and I spent several days sorting and classifying them. Then we held them in readiness, hoping for the opportunity of 'calling the bluff' of the higher intelligences. We were, as we thought, 'loaded for bear'.

Some weeks went by and nothing happened. We thought we had them stumped, and then one morning at 6:00 AM, the phone rang. It was the man's wife calling, 'Come over, quick!' she said. 'What's happened?' I asked. 'Is he still asleep?' 'Yes, but that's not it,' she replied. 'Please get over here--hurry!'

We dressed like volunteer firemen and arrived out of breath. She led us to the desk in his study and picked up a voluminous manuscript of 472 pages, written in his own hand. I said, 'Where did this come from? She said, 'I don't know. He made some strange noises in his sleep and woke me up, and I saw it here on the desk.' I asked, 'Has he been out of bed?' She said, 'Not to my knowledge. I don't see how he could have gotten out without waking me--and he's not awake yet.' I said, 'Is this his handwriting?' She said, 'It's his handwriting all right--but I don't see how he could have done it.'

I took a look at the manuscript and saw to my great astonishment that it was the answer to all of the questions that had been formulated by ourselves in our Forum group![166]

1929 Dr. Sadler explained, that many of the sessions with the sleeping subject were attended by a stenographer, who took extensive notes. Why was a stenographer necessary if the Papers just appeared out of nowhere one day or if the sleeping subject was writing messages?

1929 Dr. Sadler said, "This man is utterly unconscious, wholly oblivious to what takes place, and, unless told about it subsequently, never knows that he has been used..."

1955 Sir Hubert Wilkins makes a clarification, "The texts of the papers were spoken by the revelators through a man in his sleep and who, to this day has no idea that he was the medium.

---

[166]Sherman, p.65

Learning that the man was 'talking in his sleep' it was arranged to have a stenographer record the statements." (see p. 87)

"From first to last, when the Papers appeared, the questions disappeared."

Is it being insinuated that the Papers materialized instantaneously in place of the questions that dematerialized? This is the idea expressed by Bill Sadler, Jr.

Following are three different stories explaining the reception of the Urantia Papers, as presented by persons who were involved with the Urantia Papers. Which sounds most reasonable to you?

1. The completed Papers just suddenly appeared one day. – Bill Sadler, Jr., 1962.

2. A man in his sleep wrote the papers. – Dr. William Sadler, 1942.

3. The Papers accumulated over many years in responses to questions that were asked verbally to the sleeping subject, who responded verbally, and whose statements were recorded by a stenographer who took abundant notes. – Sir Hubert Wilkins, 1955.

"This was the procedure followed throughout the <u>many years</u> of the reception of the Urantia Papers." [emphasis mine]

Dr. Sadler explains that the procedure took many years. Sir Hubert Wilkins appears to agree with this, as he states: "The mass of the information in the Book is at first bewildering. To most of us it came piece by piece and was not so overwhelming." [167]

"No questions -- no papers."

Similarly, with the Cayce readings, if no questions were asked, no information was given.

After the first Paper was received, how did the Forum decide what questions they should ask next to the sleeping subject?

<u>1962</u> Bill Sadler, Jr., "These papers were read to the Forum. At the end of each original paper was a note suggesting the next title on which the questions should be asked. "

<u>1924</u> At the end of a reading dated October 10, 1924, the stenographer had recorded the sleeping Cayce's final statement, "We will give you the next question to ask."

---

[167]Grierson, p.202

The Forum Becomes a Closed Group

<u>1925</u> About this time, the Forum, as it were, was taken away from us. We were instructed to form a "closed group" -- requiring each member to sign a pledge of secrecy and to discuss the Papers and all matters pertaining thereto with only those persons who were members of the Forum.

Membership tickets were issued and the Charter membership numbered Thirty. The date of this organization was September, 1925. Seventeen of these Charter members are still living.

<u>1926 or 1927</u> After about twenty years of contact experience they received a challenge to ask questions of greater import. Thereafter, the first Urantia Paper began. But the Forum became a closed group in 1925, before the first Paper began! Why?

<u>1924</u> The American Medical Association became aware of doctors in Chicago using Cayce's readings to treat medical problems for their patients. Therefore, they issued a bulletin threatening expulsion of any fellow who was involved in such practice.[168]

<u>1906</u> Dr. Sadler was very sensitive to the rulings of the AMA, as he revealed when he left Chicago to circumvent the AMA.[169] They enforced a strict rule against doctors speaking in public about health issues, considered by them to be a form of advertising. Dr. Sadler began to give health lectures for

---

[168] *The Complete Edgar Cayce Readings*, Document #3780, 0254-001 Reports, (2/23/11).
[169] Meussling, 1.

Chautauqua in cities that were distant from Chicago. It was during this year that he encountered the sleeping subject for the first time.

<u>1925</u> Perhaps Dr. Sadler's fear of expulsion from the AMA motivated him to require that members of his Forum sign pledges of secrecy, in order to protect his professional standing. The alternative was that he could discontinue his research or leave Chicago again. But he had established his business and residence at 533 Diversey Parkway. If he left town again, he would have to leave his associates, his property, and his livelihood.

> **The individuals charged with the responsibility of gathering up the questions and comparing the type- written text with the original <u>handwritten</u> manu- script...** [emphasis mine]

Was the handwritten manuscript in the handwriting of the sleeping subject?

<u>1962</u> Bill Sadler, Jr. said: "All written in pencil, yes. <u>All</u> written in the handwriting of this individual, who ruefully remarked "If they ever want to draw on my bank account, I'm a dead duck because the bank will pay that signature!"

Conversely, according to Dr. Meredith Sprunger and Mark Kulieke, Dr. Sadler claimed that he called in handwriting experts who determined that the handwriting was not that of sleeping subject.

<u>1929</u> Dr. Sadler revealed that a stenographer attended the ses- sions and took extensive and abundant handwritten notes.

<u>1955</u> Sir Hubert Wilkins said, "The texts of the papers were <u>spoken</u> by the revelators through a man in his sleep and who to this day has no idea that he was the medium. Learning that the

man was 'talking in his sleep' it was arranged to have a stenographer record the statements." (see p. 87) [emphasis mine]
...came to be known as the "Contact Commissioners."

(See p. 140 for the names of the Contact Commissioners.)

<u>1927</u> **From that date forward only these Contact Commissioners attended "Contacts" and received written
communications through the contact personality.**

Mark Kulieke says, "Someone other than the sleeping subject, who was also a member of the Contact Commission,
received inner impulses of words and meanings which <u>he</u> wrote
down, which could not be heard or noticed by others. This
seems to be how some of the instructions came." [170] [emphasis
mine]
If this is true, it would explain why, even though there was a
stenographer writing notes, other handwritten messages were
appearing.

**From time to time new members were received into
the Forum, after being interviewed by the officers and
after signing the same pledge that was signed by the
original Charter Members. This pledge read: "We
acknowledge our pledge of secrecy, renewing our
promise not to discuss the Urantia Revelations or their
subject matter with any one save active Forum
members, and to take no notes of such matter as is
read or discussed at the public sessions, or make
copies or notes of what we personally read."**

The last meeting of the Forum as a genetic assembly was held on May 31st, 1942. During the 17 years

---

[170] Kulieke, 5.

of official existence the Forum attained a total membership of 486. From this date in 1942 the Forum continued as a study group to the time of the organization of the First Urantia Society.

During the period of the reception of the Urantia Papers upward of 300 different persons participated in asking these genetic questions. With but <u>a few exceptions</u>, all of the Urantia Papers were given in response to such questions. [emphasis mine]

How many is 'a few' and where and how did these 'few exceptions' originate?

In a letter to Sir Hubert Wilkins on December 16, 1950, Harold Sherman wrote, "We still feel that parts of this book have been humanly tampered with."[171] Again on February 10, 1957 he wrote, "I know that some of the material did not come from the original source."[172]

Cayce sometimes recommended books and authors while in trance. This helps explain how additional material could have been gathered from various source books, and thereby explains why some of the material "did not come from the original source."

---

[171] Wilkins Archives, box 12, folder 42 -- letter from Sherman to Wilkins dated 12/16/1950.
[172] Wilkins Archives, box 13, folder 5 -- letter from Sherman to Wilkins dated 2/10/1957.

Receiving the Completed Papers

In a way, there was a third presentation. After receiving these 196 Papers, we were told that the "Revelatory Commission" would be pleased to have us go over the Papers once more and ask questions concerning the "Clarification of Concepts" and the "Removal of Ambiguities." This program again covered several years. During this period very little new information was imparted. Only minor changes were made in any of the Papers. <u>Some matter was added - - some removed</u> -- but there was little revision or amplification of the text. [emphasis mine]

How much is some? Who added it? Why was some matter deleted? Harry Loose commented that he was very disturbed by Sadler's discarding of material.[173]

The process of compiling the Urantia manuscript followed a pattern. The questions were asked to the sleeping subject and the answers were recorded in short hand, then typed.
The forces speaking through the sleeping subject would review the manuscript as it was compiled and would make editorial suggestions.

In a similar manner, the forces speaking through the sleeping Cayce reviewed manuscripts instantaneously and made editorial suggestions. This is recorded many times in the readings! Here are a few examples:

> You will have before you the work, a copy of [manuscript by HLC] which I hold in my hand…you will tell us if this is

---

[173]Gardner, p.151

correct...and advise as to what changes or additions should be made...[174]

(Q) Please examine and criticize the outline for "There is a River:", held in my hand.
(A) As to the outline, it is, as we find, very good.[175]

(Q) Have you any further comment on this manuscript that would be helpful?[176]

(Q) How about the manuscript. Is it OK? [177]

(Q) What would you advise me regarding my manuscript...?
(A) Prepare same. Give-Give-ever showing, ever making for an opening of the door...[178]

These requests for editorial assistance were followed by suggestions from the forces that spoke through the sleeping Cayce. These are just a few of the many examples that could have been shown. But those presented are enough to establish proof that the forces speaking through Cayce, as with the sleeping subject and the Urantia material, reviewed manuscripts and made editorial suggestions.

---

[174] *The Complete Edgar Cayce Readings*, Document #8414, 0294-145 Text, #4, (6/25/32).

[175] *The Complete Edgar Cayce Readings*, Document #56954, 5749-011 Text, (9/29/39).

[176] *The Complete Edgar Cayce Readings*, Document #25718, 1135-007 Text, #12, (11/19/36).

[177] *The Complete Edgar Cayce Readings*, Document #22186, 0900-344 Text, #1, (10/8/27).

[178] *The Complete Edgar Cayce Readings*, Document #19046, 0774-005 Text, #37, (4/17/36).

Reason for Silence Respecting Details of the
Origin of *The Urantia Book*

Among the <u>several reasons</u> given us <u>at the time we were requested not to discuss the details</u> of our personal experiences associated with the origin of *The Urantia Book*, the two major reasons were the following: [emphasis mine]

The time was 1925 when the Forum was requested not to discuss the details of the origin of *The Urantia Book*. It is revealed that there were several reasons for silence, but only two are listed. Was the third reason the fear of the AMA?

1. **Unknown Features. There is much connected with the appearance of the Urantia Papers which no human being fully understands. None of us really knows just how this phenomenon was executed. There are numerous missing links in our understanding of how this revelation came to appear in written English.**

2. **The main reason for not revealing the identity of the "Contact Personality" is that the Celestial Revelators do not want any human being -- any human name -- ever to be associated with *The Urantia Book*. They want this revelation to stand on its own declarations and teachings. They are determined that future generations shall have the book wholly free from all mortal connections -- they do not want a Saint Peter, Saint Paul, Luther, Calvin, or Wesley.**

The above 'reason' is not recorded anywhere in *The Urantia Book*. But the Cayce readings advised that Cayce's name should not be used. In several of the Cayce readings, it was asked if Cayce's name should be used in conjunction with a product resulting from the reading. The answer was no. In one case it was connected to an article being submitted to a magazine, with editorial advice being requested of Cayce in trance.[179] At another time, a reading was taken to seek advice on how to distribute pharmaceutical preparations as given in the readings. The reading advised against using Cayce's name in conjunction with these products.[180] In another instance, the question was asked:

> Would an article appearing in a magazine of large circula-
> tion, and bringing Mr. Cayce's name before the public, be
> beneficial to the work which he is doing, or would it be
> harmful, in that it would tend to overload him with work?
>
> Answer: Use no name, as given. Let the work speak for
> itself, for it has been said: "He that hath seen me hath seen
> the Father." Also, "if ye believe not in me, believe in the
> work for the work's sake." Let the benefits to mankind, to
> individuals, to the entity personal, be in that vein, see?[181]

In yet another case, instructions were given not to use Cayce's name during a radio broadcast conducted by Harold Sherman and Hugh Lynn Cayce:

> There must not be used the name of the individual from
> whom such is obtained; but rather the good which may be
> gained in the experience of individuals through informa-
> tion of the psychic nature as to their qualifications or as to

---

[179] *The Complete Edgar Cayce Readings*, Document #46546, 3976-012 Text, #19, (8/25/33).

[180] *The Complete Edgar Cayce Readings*, Document #2734, 0165-017, #31, (11/16/29)

[181] *The Complete Edgar Cayce Readings*, Document #3902, 0254-032 Text, #13, (8/28/26).

the development into their activities FROM such information.[182]

The focus of the readings was upon the information, not upon the person through whom the information came. However, the readings never said to keep Cayce's identity a secret. In the same way, *The Urantia Book* does not state that the identity of the human author should be kept secret, even though it is clear that the emphasis is on the information and not the person involved.

---

[182] *The Complete Edgar Cayce Readings*, Document #4186, 0254-103 Text, (10/31/38).

How We Got the Urantia Papers

Just about all that is known or could be told about the origin of the Urantia Papers is to be found, here and there, in *The Urantia Book*. A list of such references is to be found on the back of the dust jacket of the Book.

Let us take a brief look at these citations.

1. **Page 1, par. 2. This passage refers to the difficulty of presenting expanded spiritual concepts when restricted to circumscribed human language, such as English.**

The Cayce readings state that higher dimensional realities cannot be easily expressed in three-dimensional terms.[183]

3. **Page 17, par. 1. In presenting this revelation of augmented spiritual values and universe meanings, more than one thousand human concepts were drawn from the minds of human beings of the present and the past.**

From the readings:

Edgar Cayce's mind is amenable to suggestion, the same as all other subconscious minds, but in addition thereto it has the power to interpret to the objective mind of others what it acquires from the subconscious mind of other individuals of the same kind. The subconscious mind forgets nothing. The conscious mind receives the impression from without and

---

[183] *The Complete Edgar Cayce Readings*, Document #4028, 0254-063 Reports, (4/26/32).

transfers all thought to the subconscious, where it remains
even though the conscious be destroyed. The subconscious
mind of Edgar Cayce is in direct communication with all other
subconscious minds, and is capable of interpreting through his
subconscious mind and imparting impressions received to
other objective minds, gathering in this way all knowledge
possessed by millions of other subconscious minds.[184]
[emphasis mine]

Also from the readings:

These sources may be more clearly understood by dividing
them as follows:

The subconscious minds of other individuals in the earth
plane.

The subconscious minds of discarnate entities in the spirit
plane in any of the spheres of development. [185]

**5. Page 1109, par. 4. Revelators are seldom at liberty
to anticipate scientific discoveries.**

The Cayce readings also refer to such laws, which place a
restriction on revealed knowledge. See p. 149 for further discussion of these laws.

**10. Page 1003, par. 3.   The Urantia Revelation is
unique in that it is presented by multiple authors.**

The Urantia Book was described as "a religious work of
many authors of whom Wilkins was one," by author John
Grierson. The *Spiritual Fellowship Journal* reveals many of

[184] *The Complete Edgar Cayce Readings*, Document #57044, 5756-001
Reports, (11/1/24).
[185] *The Complete Edgar Cayce Readings*, Document #8360, 0294-131 Reports,
(1/25/32).

the authors whose books were used for source material in the compilation of *The Urantia Book*.

According to Grierson, "A prayer Wilkins once wrote revealed how he thought about the spiritual meaning of life:

> My Father, I beseech
> Support in my desire to worship
> To enjoy privilege without abuse
> To have liberty without license
> To have power, and refuse to use it for self aggran-
> dizement..."

Most of this poem is used in Paper 48 of *The Urantia Book*:

> To enjoy privilege without abuse,
> to have liberty without license,
> to possess power and steadfastly refuse to use it for
> self-aggrandizement...[186]

***

This has been my attempt to bring together all of the information concerning the origin of the Urantia material, fill in the missing pieces with information gathered elsewhere, and to ask some of the questions that must have occurred in the minds of others before me. My conclusions may not be decisive for anyone. They make sense to me. There is perhaps additional information somewhere that will eventually surface to give a clearer picture of the events covered in this section.

---

[186] *The Urantia Book*, 556, #6.

2. The Bill Sadler, Jr. Tape

Following is the first recorded interview of the origin of the Urantia Papers. It is typed in bold print, in deposition form, and reads exactly as it sounds on tape. The tape was digitized by sophisticated state of the art computer equipment to eliminate the hum and static of the original tape recorder. Following is an exact reproduction of the William (Bill) Sadler, Jr. interview tape. David Kantor has placed an introduction at the beginning of the interview.

***

Hello, this is David Kantor. The tape you are about to hear was given to me by Berkley Elliott in 1994, with a request that I not make its existence known until after she had died. It contains the voice of Bill Sadler, Jr. describing some of the details of the way *The Urantia Book* came into being. It was recorded after a study group in the home of Berkley Elliott on February 18, 1962 [at approximately 9:30 P.M.]. There is a great deal of background noise on the original tape that I did not attempt to remove. I hope you find this interesting and informative.

***

Man #1: I, I would just like to ask, ah, some, ah, ah, you know -- gimme a brief un-na, I don't want to take any time, ju, just a little break now, just briefly, you know.

Bill Sadler, Jr.: What do you want to know?

Man #1: Well, I want to know, uh, how it began and, uh, who wrote it, uh, the authority and, uh, so on.

Bill Sadler, Jr.: Sadler, Bill, Flooded room.

After listening to Bill's comment carefully many times, I asked Matthew Block what he thought Bill was saying, when he said what sounded like 'flooded room'. Matthew thinks the statement made was "Let it run."

> **Man #2: 'Ere you go, 'ere you go again le lee, heh, heh...**

I could not understand this remark. Matthew had no idea either.

> **Bill Sadler, Jr.: [short silence] Well, it began a long time ago. [long pause] It began, uh, oh, it has it roots back ... 40 years ago.**

Bill is referring to the beginning of the Forum, which began in 1923. But Sadler first discovered the sleeping subject in 1906.

> **Bill Sadler, Jr.: [someone coughs] If you'll read this book ... loan me yours will ya? I need a cover ... ah, [someone coughs] the back of this dust jacket [someone coughs] says: Concerning the nature and origin of organization of *The Urantia Book*. And if you read, uh, four out of the thirteen references here it refers to a person, a human being, who was concerned in the origin of this book. If you'll read the book farther you will see to it, you will see that this human being at no point makes any claim to having written any part of this book. He was involved ... in its origin.**

"The text of the papers were spoken by the revelators through a man in his sleep and who to this day <u>has no idea that he was the</u>

medium," Sir Hubert Wilkins, 11/5/55 (see p. 87).   It is
therefore not surprising that the man made no claim to having
written any part of this book. [emphasis mine]

> **Bill Sadler, Jr.: [pause] The ... book ... claims to be,
> flatly, a revelation. There's a statement made in the
> signature of the first paper, which is unequivocal,
> and this 'tag-n-na-fron-idn't-straddle.'**

I believe what Bill said was "This tag in the front isn't straddle." What he probably meant was that the author of this paper
was not 'straddling the fence'.

> **Bill Sadler, Jr. [pause] This, the author of this
> paper, on page 32, identifies himself as a Divine
> Counselor. He said, "I am commissioned to spon-
> sor those papers portraying the nature and attrib-
> utes of God because I represent the highest source
> of information available for such a purpose on any
> inhabited world. I have served as a Divine Coun-
> selor in all seven of the superuniverses and have
> long resided at the Paradise center of all things.
> Many times have I enjoyed the supreme pleasure of
> a sojourn in the immediate personal presence of the
> Universal Father. I portray the reality and truth of
> the   Father's   nature   and   attributes   with
> unchallengeable authority; I know whereof I
> speak." [pause] You can say, uh, "nonsense," but
> at least you can't say, you can't say the man is
> straddling.**

The use here of the word 'straddling' confirms the former
interpretation of the use of the word 'straddle'.

> **[pause]
> Man #1: I can, I can only say the, uh, there's some-
> thing that, uh, Jesus said, you know?**

Bill Sadler, Jr.: What was that?

Man #1: Ye shall know the truth.

Bill Sadler, Jr.: That's right.

Another man's voice: see-kahn-ah...

Mark Kulieke wrote to me and said he thinks this man said, "Seek and", as in 'seek and ye shall find.'

> **Bill Sadler, Jr.: Now, [long pause - silence - someone coughs] many years ago [long pause] my parents, who were physicians, had brought to their attention the individual who's referred to in this [someone coughs] book. In one of the books my father wrote he made mention of this case, in an Appendix at the tail end of the book, The [someone coughs] *Mind at Mischief* which was published in the 1920's. My father, in his solid days, had as a hobby spook hunting. He was an exposer of mediums. His two running mates were the head of the department of psychology at Northwestern University...**

One of these "running mates" was probably Robert H. Gault, Professor of Psychology, Northwestern University, who wrote the Introduction for *The Mind at Mischief*.

> **Bill Sadler, Jr.: ... and Howard Thurston, a professional magician. When you take a psychologist, a physician and a magician and put them together -- God help the medium!**

Man's laughter: heh, heh.

Bill does not mention Harry Houdini. This is probably because Bill was in Nicaragua fighting in a war from 1924 to 1928. Dr. Sadler called in Houdini to observe the sleeping subject sometime after 1924 and before October 1926.

Bill Sadler, Jr.: Ah, there's a book, out-of-print now, which my father wrote, called *The Truth About Spiritualism*, in which he identifies so-called spiritualists as falling in one of two categories -- they either are practicing fraud deliberately, for gain or glory or both, or they are self-deceived. [pause] I think in that book he says with one possible exception. [pause] These two physicians became interested in this case.

The one exception was the sleeping subject who channeled the Urantia material.

Bill Sadler, Jr.: This man would go to sleep and he'd talk [pause] and, uh, what came out was intriguing ... and different.

What came out of the sleeping Cayce was also intriguing and different. This is what set him apart from other mediums of his day.

Bill Sadler, Jr.: He was never interested in helping you find Ed Mahoochy's watch that had been lost. Ah, he was never interested in telling you what the stock market was going to do, or anything else that was particularly practical.

Once, Cayce believed he had lost his gift forever, through his own "wrongheadedness". It disappeared for what turned into an entire year after he had joined an associate in the venture of using it to predict horse races in order to raise money to replace his burned down photography studio. Many times

Cayce was troubled by headaches and low spirits, in the early years, after readings which he later found that others had used to make money instead of to secure the medical counsel which he thought he was giving. For these reasons Cayce was not interested in locating lost treasure, predicting horse races, or the stock market.

> **Bill Sadler, Jr.: Ah, you never had a chance to talk to your Uncle George ... who passed on.**

Within the readings, Cayce continually warned against communication with the dead.[187]

> **Bill Sadler, Jr.: And, uh, in other words this was distinctly offbeat, you follow me? [pause] At about this time ... a Sunday afternoon group came to be organized in Chicago, at our house. It came about when my father was giving a commencement address, I was in high school then. He was giving a commencement at Ames Col--, at, at Ames, Iowa at Iowa State. He wrote me a letter, and he says, "You know, son," he said, "we don't, we're religious people but we're not church members." And he said "I think Sundays should be productive, as well as a day of rest." He said "What do you say if we invited in our friends and we had a discussion group and we talked about, well, kind of a forum -- talk about health and disease and politics and philosophy, sociology, history and what have you." That group came into existence I think in the year 1922. I found that letter some years ago and it's in the archives, I hope preserved, 'cause it's the original charter of the Chicago Forum. [short**

---

[187] Furst, 302.

pause] In the course of time this group became interested in spiritualism. Pop was writing his book on spiritualism and what more natural than they would discuss, ah, "Well, what did you find out?" My dad was ah, humorously mischievous. Ah, he went to a vaudeville show at McVicar's in the -- they had vaudeville in those days -- and there was a mind-reading act on, [cough] and, uh, Pop attended twice, held conference with his friends and they decid'd-ta work with a pair of wire clippers, and he clipped the wire that was hooking up the guy in the audience with a gal on the stage, at which point she fainted. "Is there a physician in the house?" and he had the gall to go back and take care of her.

[Extreme laughter from the listeners]

Bill Sadler, Jr.: The ... [coughing]. In their discussions -- now, what I'm telling you for a little bit in through here is hearsay, because at about this time I was in Nicaragua fightin' a revolution and ah, kind 'a grew up with a queer notion that a lad was not a man until he'd been blooded. And you have no idea how difficult it was to find a war, in the 1920's. I searched and searched and finally found one. It was a nice war, too -- the last real good one. [cough] Kind of like a quail shoot - [wheezing laughter] - except the quail could shoot back.

Um, from 1924 until 1928 [coughing] I'll tell you hearsay. Prior to this time and subsequent to 1928 I'll give you direct, first-hand information. The question came up "Well, uh, are all such phenomena fraudulent?" Well, ah, my father was an honest guy -- he said, "Well there's one case," he said, "that's very puzzled." "Well tell us about it."

So, the Forum became intrigued with the short-hand notes that had been taken on things which this medium would talk about. [coughing]

"Learning that this man was 'talking in his sleep' it was arranged to have a stenographer record the statements," Sir Hubert Wilkins, 11/5/55 (see p. 87 for complete quote).

Bill Sadler, Jr.: Very. Very intriguing case, they're all now burned. [pause] And that was the condition of affairs when, on one evening when, uh, they were talking to this chap ... a kindofa argument came up. Someone was talking who claimed to be a mighty messenger. And he was challenged, "Can you prove you're a mighty messenger?" "No," he said, "of course not -- and you can't prove I'm not either. But," he said, "if you knew what I knew you wouldn't ask these sort of half-baked questions. You would prepare some of the most deep, far-reaching and searching questions that could ever be asked."

From Dr. Sadler's Papers:

After about twenty years of contact experience, an alleged student-visitor, speaking through this sleeping subject during one of these nocturnal vigils, in answer to one of our questions, said: "If you only knew what you are in contact with you would not ask such trivial questions. You would rather ask such questions as might elicit answers of supreme value to the human race."[188]

---

[188] This is from Dr. Sadler's papers, section: "How the Urantia Papers Started," see p. 198.

Dr. Sadler's first encounter with the sleeping subject was in 1906. In a reading given in early 1927, (about twenty years after 1906) Cayce challenged his listeners to ask more significant questions when he said: "Why is such communication so often of seemingly an unnecessary nature? ... Rather cultivate that of such communications, and receive the answer to that of the most profound that may be propounded," A.R.E. document 5756-004, dated 3/17/27.

> **Bill Sadler, Jr.: Well, my father is half-English and half-Irish, and, uh, you can get a reserved, uh, reaction from him, or you can get damn mad. He got damn mad on this occasion, and he says this is, this is ridiculous" -- He said "We're supposed to be checking out phenomena and," he said, "we're challenged! " He said, "Let's, let's take him up on it." So the next Sunday when the Forum met, they came in on the deal. And I think -- I'm told -- that approximately 5,000 questions were assembled, many of them duplicates, some of them undoubtedly silly -- Who created God? How old is God? -- these are unanswerable questions. I haven't the foggiest notion of what was expected to transpire. Maybe they thought they were going over at sometime and read all these questions and take down the answers in shorthand.**
>
> **But what happened was this: One day the questions were gone, and where the papers had been kept was the first of the Urantia Papers, entitled "The Universal Father." [pause]**

If this is true and the Urantia Papers just suddenly appeared in place of some questions which were written down and kept somewhere, why would a stenographer be necessary? Why would an unconscious man be necessary to talk in his sleep? Why not just write down some more questions and place the questions in the same place and wait for more completed papers to appear?

Since Dr. Sadler stated in 1929, that a stenographer was frequently in attendance and took voluminous notes, it seems logical that the sleeping subject was talking.

> **Bill Sadler, Jr.: Now, [pause] I'll tell you how I think this paper was written. And my theory is not 100% correct, but it's the best I can devise, so I share it with you. It's the most acceptable to me. It explains 97% of the problem, and I won't even get into the other 3%, we'll forget it. This is the theory I accept. I want you to visualize several points in space -- geographic locations -- like, uh, the skirt on Ophell, Berk Elliott's place where you meet on Wednesday night here in Oklahoma City. We'll call them point A, point B, point C and point D. I think the papers were dictated, or conceived, at point A. And I think if we could have been present at point A when any one of these papers were being written, we would have seen absolutely nothing. At point A was perhaps this Divine Counselor who signs Paper One. [cough] He is presenting his concepts in the language of Uversa. There's a translator there, who translates Uversa into Salvington. There's another translator who translates Salvington into Satania. There's another translator who translates Satania into English. You cannot translate from Uversa into English, the languages are too far apart.**

Dr. Gina Cerminara, Ph.D., writes about these types of translation difficulties with respect to the information coming through the sleeping Cayce in an article entitled "The Language of the Cayce Readings" (see p. 14 for details). Her conclusion is that the language of the readings sounds as if it is coming from a very knowledgeable person from an ancient time, who is trying to compress unlimited knowledge into three dimensional terms, portraying complex ideas to ordinary people, using a foreign language.

Bill Sadler, Jr.: And I suspect 99% + of the original concept was lost in translation. English is too primitive a language. How would you operate in, let's say Bantu, where the, where thee arithmetical system is [cough] 1, 2, 3, many. That's the end of your numbers. How would you deal with large systems? You se - you see the problem? I think point A was linked by some kind of a circuit -- a communication circuit, not a wire -- but a, s-, some circuit over which intelligence could flow to point B. [someone clears their throat] Now you'd have something to see at point B, but it would be very dull. It would be a man asleep, somerryory looking guy, just asleep, doing nothing. Now, if you could get to point C [Bill's voice raises to a moderately higher pitch briefly] this would be exciting! You member on the day of the resurrection, the soldiers sold, saw the stone roll away, apparently by itself? And they took out double time or triple time for Jerusalem? Now that stone was being pushed. It was being pushed by some secondary midwayers, who are non-corporeal beings who can deal with physical substances. At point C I think you'd 'ave seen a very exciting phenomena -- a pencil moving over paper with no visible means of propulsion. [pause - silence] That's where the physical writing was consummated.

If a pencil was moving across a paper by itself to write the Urantia Papers, why would an unconscious talking man and a stenographer be involved at all?

Bill Sadler, Jr.: And then there's one more point, point B, where we found the papers. [pause] Now

[pause] all during these years ... this particular individual, who is referred to in this book, was never seen to write one of these papers. [pause] And don't think that we weren't wearing gumshoes looking. [pause] If he wrote them, all I can say is he was more clever than the whole lot of us -- he was never observed to write them.

These papers were read to the Forum. At the end of each original paper was a note suggesting the next title on which the questions should be asked.

At the end of a Cayce reading, dated October 10, 1924, the stenographer's last note on the page recorded the forces speaking through the sleeping Cayce: "We will give you the next question to ask."

Bill Sadler, Jr.: This is how they led us through the first time. The papers were read to the Forum, they generated more questions, and over a period of years this [Sadler slaps his book] book accumulated. And eventually, when we had money enough, we published it. In nineteen hundred fifty [cough] uh, we completed the preparation of our plates. As money came in, uh, we forecast inflation, this was pretty obvious. And so we took the hard dollars we got and we spent them as quickly as we could with, with - uh - the Donnelly Company. We picked the Donnelly, one, because they're Chicago, two, they've got a good reputation for handling India paper, and not all printers can handle India paper, it's tricky. Uh, if you went to Chicago you could search out the records of the County Clerk and you would find that the Urantia Foundation was established in nineteen hundred fifty. It was established by the anonymous donation [bell dings] of the plates [someone coughs -- pause] for *The Urantia Book*. You see we've improved on the

moral. Joe Smith got gold plates, but we got nickel, uh, nickel-plated stereotypes that you buckle right on the press 'n' you print 16 pages. These plates are much more useful.

You [cough] could go to Donnelly's 'n' say, "Who, ah, who did you negotiate with?" They'd say "a chap by the name of W.C. Kellogg." And you would say "Well, where is he?" - "Well, he's dead."

This is a reference to Wilfred Custer Kellogg, who was Lena Sadler's cousin and William Sadler's brother-in-law by marriage. Wilfred died after the publication of *The Urantia Book.*

Bill Sadler, Jr.: So that source of the information is gone. The Urantia Foundation, uh, owns the copyright to this book. There are five trustees of the Urantia Foundation -- I'm one, of these five. Uh, [pause] in about nineteen hundred and fifty four, [someone coughs] these five trustees selected thirty-six people from this Forum. And these thirty-six people organized the Urantia Brotherhood. This group here is one of the component societies of the Urantia Brotherhood. [pause] The book was published in October of 1955 and it has been present ever since. How we got it, Berk, natural. [cough] This, this story which I have told to you is a direct, first-hand story, except for the years 1924-1928, what I've told you, what I've learned, and what's important. Otherwise, I'm giving you first-hand information. [pause - silence - clinking ice] And that's the first time that story's ever been recorded.

Male listener: Ah, just what I was gonna ask you.

Bill Sadler, Jr.: Umhmm.

Male listener: Can we change it -- I was talking with Helen, that, that was the first time it ever went on tape.

Bill Sadler, Jr.: That's right.

Woman: Was the singrayup again, in the written identifiable as a local person [man belches] for the society or anything?

Bill Sadler, Jr.: We did all the things that curious human beings would do.

[Group laughter]

Bill Sadler, Jr.: And we were consistently baffled.

Woman: Were they all written in pencil?

Bill Sadler, Jr.: All written in pencil, yes. [Bill coughs] All written in the handwriting of this individual, who ruefully remarked "If they ever want to draw on my bank account I, I'm a dead duck because the [humorously] b-bank will pay that signature."

According to Dr. Sadler and Wilkins, a stenographer took notes of everything that was spoken by this sleeping subject.

In *Birth of a Revelation*, the author states that Dr. Sadler had handwriting experts come in and examine the handwriting that was allegedly written by the sleeping subject. The result was, according to Dr. Sadler, that the handwriting was not that of the sleeping subject.

Man: With him at all time prob'ly embarrassed him to take it apart.

Bill Sadler, Jr.: Yes. [pause] The next question you should ask is "Who is this guy?"

[Group laughter]

Woman: Next question.

Man: You know, I, I had dismissed that, uh ...

Bill Sadler, Jr.: Well, I don't answer that anyway. [chuckles from listeners] I took an oath many years ago never to divulge who he is. Now that oath was required of me and all other persons who know his identity, by the [pause] Commissioner who sponsored the last of these papers.

There were two categories of commissioners involved with the Urantia Papers: human and superhuman. The first was the human (or corporeal) Contact Commissioners and the second was the group of non-corporeal beings who presented the Urantia information through the sleeping subject.

It is reasonable to assume that whoever the commissioner was that Bill was referring to -- he was around prior to September 1925 (since that was the date secrecy began) -- and still around during the last papers, which Bill says he sponsored. Was this unidentified commissioner corporeal or non-corporeal?

The Urantia Book lists the non-corporeal commissioners who sponsored the last papers as being twelve Urantia mid-wayers and a Melchizedek. These particular commissioners weren't present sponsoring papers in 1925.

The first 31 papers were sponsored by a commission consisting of 24 non-corporeal Orvonton administrators, none of whom was a midwayer or a Melchizedek. These Orvonton commissioners were no longer present when the last papers were created.

The only commissioners who were involved in every phase of the process, from beginning to end, were the human commissioners. The logical conclusion is that the commissioner who required the oath of secrecy was human!

The human Contact Commissioners were Dr. William Sadler, Dr. Lena Sadler, Bill Sadler, Jr., Emma Christensen, Wilfred Kellogg, and Anna Kellogg.

Whoever the unidentified human commissioner was, to whom Bill was referring, he possessed the authority among the group of contact commissioners to demand oaths of secrecy from the rest of them.

> **Bill Sadler, Jr.: Uh, we think we know why it was required. We think we would have required it of each other had it not been required of us. We think this individual would have asked us to maintain secrecy had no one else asked us. [cough]**

Bill reveals that the sleeping subject never asked to remain unknown. In fact, Wilkins revealed that the man never even knew he was used as the medium. The secrecy may have been requested by Dr. William Sadler (who was a 'Commissioner') due to professional ethics of confidentiality and/or because in August of 1924, the American Medical Association became aware of doctors in Chicago using Cayce's readings to diagnose medical problems for their patients. Therefore, they issued a bulletin threatening expulsion of any fellow who was involved in such practice (see p. 20 for details).

> **Bill Sadler, Jr.: You see, uh, this chap, I think, was picked for this job, as you'll read in here, first because of the qualifications of his Thought Adjuster. His is an experienced thought adjuster. Secondly, because he's got a passion for anonymity —**

Cayce never made any public demonstrations of his power and he never sought any publicity.[189]

> -- he's a very stable guy. He is the exact opposite of the type of guy you'd think would be associated with this. [Bill clears his throat] Many years ago, I first met Meredith Sprunger who's a very nice guy. He teaches at a college at Fort Wayne and he's got the faculty involved in this book now. And, uh, when I met Meredith he was hot as a firecracker, he had to know wh-, who, who this man was. Well, I met Meredith through Judge Hammerschmidt of Fort, of, uh, South Bend, and Judge Hammerschmidt learned about it from Will Hara. Will Hara [with affection] a great guy. He died in 80, mid-90 -- about, uh, 5 years ago -- he was like a one-horse shay. Until 3 months before his death he was in pretty good shape and then he just disintegrated and died quickly. Will Hara was one of the fore-founders of the National Standard Company. And when I knew him he was honorary chairman. A, uh, uh, trangley guy, a tough businessman, and, uh, and an all-around self-made man. Uh, modest but not insignificant affairs. And I r'member when Meredith said, "Well, but I must know who this man is." And I turned and I said, Meredith, it's not Mr. Hara, but it could be.
>
> This man was poured out of the same mold -- a businessman, ...

Edgar Cayce was a businessman. He ran his own photography studio.

---

[189] Sugrue, 6.

... with his head pretty well screwed on his shoulders, his feet pretty solid on the ground, who has about the same attitude toward this whole thing as a chap would have if he were, uh, subject to mild epileptic fits -- mildly ashamed at being mixed up in a kind of a screwball, spooky thing like this.

During an interview in 1911, Cayce was asked, "Didn't it occur to you to use this power for your own advantage?" Cayce replied, "No sir, I was ashamed of it. It seemed to me that I ought not to be exhibiting myself in such a way."

Bill Sadler, Jr.: You see what a safe person this was, the exact opposite of a prophet. This I think was his principal human qualification. [cough] He doesn't want to be known. We think it's wise that he's not known, and if any of us had any doubts, an oath was required of us. We think that always in the past, the prophet has messed up the teaching. Now here's a teaching which stands with no prophet ... for the first time.

(Following the above portion of this interview, there were additional questions and answers, which in my opinion were not relevant to this literary work. Therefore, they have been omitted and this transcript continues with relevant material. Copies of the complete original tape are available upon request)

Bill Sadler, Jr.: Thee, the thing I've been watching for is archaeological work. You see, there's a gap between second Eden and our oldest city. This gap is formidable, because second Eden, uh, goes back, uh, twenty - twenty-five - thirty thousand years, and yet the oldest cities that we've identified, with one exception, uh, go back to about four-thousand to five-thousand BC. Now in the last few years a

major breakthrough has taken place in the excavations at Jericho. They used carbon-14 in dating, which is pretty accurate. There's a gal archaeologist who's done her job and she has established that Jericho goes back to about nine thousand BC.   [cough].   This is a major breakthrough. And it's all the more major because she's also established that Jericho is not the oldest city. Because on the third level of Jericho, they suddenly find sophisticated pottery which was introduced by invaders. And they know that the pottery evolved in cities which were older than Jericho. This is the first big breakthrough. And the first time that we have anything to go along with, with a site that Pompoli excavated up in Russian Turkistan, which he dates, uh, he dates the Bronze culture at nine thousand BC. This thing sort of stands out in the end. Nobody pays any attention to him - he just doesn't fit in. [Bill coughs] I think the, I think the archaeologists are gonna be commin' near it, to validating the chronology of the book. And this is the first breakthrough, and it's only three years old!

[end transcript of Bill Sadler, Jr. taped interview]

3. Other Stories Concerning *The Urantia Book*

Besides the recollections of Dr. Sadler and his son about the reception of the Urantia Papers, there are various other stories that circulate about these events. This section includes some of these, with comparable accounts regarding the Cayce sessions.

Humor

Mark Kulieke tells the reader that there was humor involved in the communication between the spiritual beings and the Contact Commission.[190]

This was also true of the forces who spoke through Edgar Cayce. They humorously said "he is thought crazy enough anyway!" [191]

Humor was ever present in the Cayce readings.[192]

(Also see *Humor From the Psychic*, by Edgar Evans Cayce, which gives many examples of humor displayed in the readings.)

Story Concerning a Safety Deposit Box

There is a story which I have heard concerning Dr. Sadler placing papers in a safety deposit box and the sleeping subject accessing the information written on the papers which he had placed there. For any of you *Urantia Book* readers who have heard that story, here is a similar story about Cayce:

---

[190] Kulieke, 6.
[191] *The Complete Edgar Cayce Readings*, Document #57094, 5756-014 Text, (7/17/34).
[192] Agee, 45.

"Father took at random a paper from his safe deposit box, sealed it in an envelope, placed it on the inside of his secret vest pocket, buttoned his coat and overcoat - and you (Edgar Cayce) told the men the contents and signatures of the document."[193]

Stories of the Identity of the Contact Person

There are various stories that have circulated about the initial beginnings of the Urantia Papers (See Sherman's book How *to Know What to Believe* and also *Urantia: The Great Cult Mystery* by Martin Gardner, for details of various stories).

In one story, a man was talking in his sleep and someone else wrote down what he said.

An alternate version stated that a man produced hundreds of hand written pages in one night, while he was unconscious.

Another account states that a young stockbroker, while unconsciousness, typed hundreds of pages on a typewriter, as his wife slept nearby, undisturbed by the typing.

Many people believe that Wilfred Kellogg was the sleeping subject. But Sadler revealed that the sleeping subject was a married individual, when Sadler first encountered him. Kellogg was not married at the time *The Urantia Book* adventure began, whether one takes 1906 or 1911 as a beginning date. However, Cayce was married in 1903.

Sadler also revealed that the sleeping subject was in the general classification of psychics and trance mediums.[194] I have not discovered any references that indicate Kellogg was a psychic or a trance medium.

---

[193] *The Complete Edgar Cayce Readings*, Document #52236, 4950-001 Reports, (1/1/00).
[194] Sadler, *Mind at Mischief*, 332.

Sadler promised that he would not publish anything about this unique case during the lifetime of the sleeping subject, but Kellogg was alive when *The Urantia Book* was published.

Comparison of Details about the Sleeping Subject

	Kellogg	**Sleeping Subject**	**Cayce**
Married by 1906	No	Yes	Yes
Married by 1911	No	Yes	Yes
Died before 1955	No	Yes	Yes
Psychic	No	Yes	Yes
Trance medium	No	Yes	Yes

Some readers of *The Urantia Book* believe that the revelators intended that the identity of the sleeping subject should never be known. Therefore, the various stories about his identity were created to disguise the actual facts. This helps explain the fabrications and the inconsistencies in the different stories. I reasoned that if any of the stories had been entirely true, there would have been only one story. To me it appeared that each rendition was constructed upon a grain of fact, and each contained a portion of truth.

Part IV: Final Comments

1. The Communications

The ways in which the communications were delivered, the types of sources from which they came, and the limitations placed on their transmittal, all converge on an event that was not only uncommon, but virtually unheard of outside of these two cases. This section gives some of the many parallels that lead, once again, to the feasible conclusion that these were not different events at all, but a very well disguised singular episode of great significance in recent history.

Mandate Limiting Revealed Knowledge

The following quotations from *The Urantia Book* illustrate the limitations placed on the revelators in passing their information to us:

> **P. 350, Par. 6:** ... we are restricted, not only by the limitations of human comprehension, but also by the terms of the mandate governing these disclosures...

> **P. 578, Para. 1:** ... we are limited by the planetary quarantine and by the system isolation. We must be guided by these restrictions in all our efforts ... but in so far as is permissible, you have been instructed...

> **P. 1109, Para. 4:** Mankind should understand that we who participate in the revelation of truth are very rigorously limited by the instructions of our superiors ... Revelators must act in accordance with the instructions which form a part of the revelation mandate ... new developments we even now foresee, but we are forbidden to include such humanly undiscovered facts in the revelatory records.

The Cayce readings also refer to such laws, which place a restriction on revealed knowledge: "Do not ever (THIS IS LAW) give any knowledge, workable or theory, for which there is not necessity of same for man's better development in earth plane."[195]

Development of Terms

While searching the Cayce readings, I discovered that the forces communicating through Cayce sometimes adopted the use of phrases which had developed during the communication process. An example of this is found in a reading that includes the insertion of a note by Gladys Davis:

> An article on IPSAB appearing in 11/72 issue of the *A.R.E. Journal* by Tom Johnson and Carol A. Barraff states: "It is not known where the name originated." [Then follows Gladys Davis, stenographer's note:] *This reminds me to make this notation: The name was suggested by Gertrude Cayce, combining the first letters of the main ingredients: iodine, prickly ash bark [or peppermint], salt. Soon the readings started using the name.*[196] [emphasis mine]

This process of developing terminology was also noted with Sadler's group, as can be seen when reading Appendix A, Dr. Sadler's papers. He said that new terms were introduced and developed during the contact sessions, terms developed over the course of the years in this manner. One such term is "Thought Adjuster". This refers to the Spark of the God that exists within each human being.

The Cayce readings also speak of the divine spark:

> That which is the active force in the animate object; that is the spark or the image of the Maker. Mind is the factor that

---

[195] *The Complete Edgar Cayce Readings*, Document #32462, 1800-002 Text, #6, (2/13/25).

[196] *The Complete Edgar Cayce Readings*, Document #32458, 1800-001 Text, end of #5, (10/17/71 G.D.'s note).

is in direct opposition of will. Mind being that control of, or being the spark of the Maker, the Will, the individual when we reach the plane of man. Mind being and is the factor governing the contention, or the interlaying space, if you please, between the physical to the soul, and the soul to the spirit forces within the individual ... to develop the entity of physical force toward the spark or infinite force, giving the life force to the body. The mind may be classified into two forces - that between the physical and soul and that between the soul and the spirit force ... the nearer approach the mind comes to the divide, between the soul and spirit forces, the nearer we become to that infinite force that guides when it is allowed to the individual's actions day by day.[197]

Living and Deceased Mortal Minds Were Sources of Information

The Urantia Book claims that more than 1,000 human concepts were used from mortals of the past and present.[198]

In *There is a River:*, Thomas Sugrue stated, "One of the sources of [Cayce's] information were millions of sub-conscious minds of human beings, though their consciousness may have been destroyed by death."

This differs from communications with 'the dead.' It refers to a generic 'pool of consciousness', which has accumulated throughout time, and combines all experiences of each human lifetime. These records of experiences are also known as the Book of Life or the akashic records.

---

[197] *The Complete Edgar Cayce Readings*, Document #45022, 3744-001 Text, #3, (10/8/23).
[198] *The Urantia Book*, 17.

The readings state, "The conscious mind receives the impressions from without and transfers all thought to the sub-conscious, where it remains even though the conscious be destroyed."[199]

From the readings:

> **Question 11**: "From what source does this body Edgar Cayce derive its information?"
>
> **Answer**: "The information as given or obtained from this body is gathered from the sources from which the suggestion may derive its information. In this state the conscious mind becomes subjugated to the subconscious, superconscious or soul mind; and may and does communicate with like minds, and the subconscious or soul force becomes universal. *From any subconscious mind information may be obtained, either from this plane or from the impressions as left by the individuals that have gone on before*, as we see a mirror reflecting direct that which is before it. It is not the object itself, but that reflected, as in this: The suggestion that reaches through to the subconscious or soul, in this state, gathers information from that as reflected from what has been or is called real or material, whether of the material body or of the physical forces, and just as the mirror may be waved or bended to reflect in an obtuse manner, so that suggestion to the soul forces may bend the reflection of that given; yet within the image itself is what is reflected and not that of some other.
>
> Through the forces of the soul, *through the mind of others as presented, or that have gone on before*; through the subjugation of the physical forces in this manner, the body obtains information."[200][emphasis mine]

---

[199] Sugrue, 154.

[200] *The Complete Edgar Cayce Readings*, Document #45026, 3744-002 Text, (10/9/23).

2. Other Similarities Regarding Cayce and *The Urantia Book*

Many similarities in the Cayce readings and *The Urantia Book* have been described throughout the chapters of this book. Following are some that have not been previously disclosed, *but there are more being discovered, even as this book goes to print!*

1. The Forum began in October, 1923. Cayce's first metaphysical reading was October, 1923.

2. The sleeping subject stated that Jesus' mission to earth was not to found a new religion. This was also clearly stated by Edgar Cayce while in trance.

3. *The Urantia Book* records that Jesus was a musician and played the harp. In June of 1932, speaking of Jesus, the sleeping Cayce said, "He is a musician and uses the harp."[201] Also in 1933 the readings stated, "The Prince of Peace (Jesus) was a harpist himself."[202]

4. *The Urantia Book* states that Christ incarnated as Melchizedek, then thousands of years later reincarnated as Jesus. The Cayce readings also record Christ incarnating as a Melchizedek and thousands of years later as Jesus.

5. The sleeping subject and the Cayce readings both state that "All force is one force."[203]

---

[201] *The Complete Edgar Cayce Readings*, Document #56914, 5749-001 Text, #13, (3/17/27).

[202] *The Complete Edgar Cayce Readings*, Document #6954, 0275-035 Text, #10, (11/21/33).

[203] Agee, 41.

6. The term 'Most High God' appears in *The Urantia Book* five times. It also appears five times in *The Complete Edgar Cayce Readings* on CD-ROM.

7. *The Urantia Book* condemns the idea of reincarnation, but supports the idea of resurrection, and evolution through rebirth. The Cayce readings explain that reincarnation and resurrection meant the same thing during the time of Jesus. A study of word origins confirmed this. The readings portray reincarnation as the process of evolution.

8. *The Urantia Book* supports the idea of the soul's continued existence of life after physical death, in a world of finer matter. The Cayce readings also reveal the continued existence of the soul after death, in a world of matter, but of finer matter.[204]

9. *The Urantia Book* states that death brings only the consciousness of survival.[205] The readings state that conditions are not changed by death.[206] Cayce indicated that more often than not, one who has passed on does not suddenly have all knowledge, but only what he had when he died.[207] In another instance, the readings state that the dead do not know a great deal more than they did while living.[208]

10. *The Urantia Book* reveals that there is an educational process involving teachers in the next life, after the soul leaves

---

[204] Agee, 44.
[205] *The Urantia Book*, 556.
[206] Agee, 41.
[207] *The Complete Edgar Cayce Readings*, Document #57044, 5756-001 Reports, 1/4/84 Gladys Davis' answer to Dr. C. Norman Shealy's letter.
[208] Bro, *Edgar Cayce on Religion and Psychic Experience*, 58.

earth and passes on.[209] Cayce's readings described classrooms in which teachers were preparing souls for their next return to earth.[210]

11. *The Urantia Book* and the Cayce readings both use the term "Light and Life."

12. In *The Urantia Book*, the Forces speaking through the sleeping subject stated that it is difficult to express higher universe concepts using human language.[211] The Forces speaking through the sleeping Cayce stated that higher dimensional realities cannot be easily expressed in three-dimensional terms.[212]

13. *The Urantia Book* records that the sleeping subject revealed that ESP is a natural phenomenon of evolution. The Cayce readings say: "The possibility of the developing of thought transference is   first being shown, evolution, you see?"[213] In *Edgar Cayce on Religion and Psychic Experience*, the author states that "a soul might expect its natural psychic ability to be enhanced by Universal Forces."[214]

14. *The Urantia Book* states that there is not one Urantia religion that could not benefit by studying the best in all other faiths, for all contain truth. The Cayce readings state, "All religious faiths have their element of truth."

---

[209] *The Urantia Book*, 554.
[210] Agee, 50.
[211] *The Urantia Book*, 1.
[212] *The Complete Edgar Cayce Readings*, Document #4028, 0254-063 Reports, 12/45 A.R.E. Bulletin article by Gina Cerminara, reprinted April 1966 in the A.R.E. Journal, entitled "The Language of the Cayce readings."
[213] *The Complete Edgar Cayce Readings*, 3744 series, readings.
[214] Bro, *Edgar Cayce on Religion and Psychic Experience*, 37.

15. *The Urantia Book* teaches that the soul never dies, but can become separated from God. If a soul continues in iniquity, eventually it will cease to exist as a separate entity and become reabsorbed back to the original source. In 1923, the question was asked Cayce: "Does the soul ever die?" The reply: "Banishment, not death."[215] And again in *Edgar Cayce on Religion and Psychic Experience*, "If a soul doesn't choose God, it is eventually reabsorbed back to its original state ... but essential above all for understanding man was the nature and work of the individual soul, which had its own mind and force. This soul was a psychological universe in itself, destined to endure for all eternity. It would either grow, through eons of time, into full, con-scious, willing partnership with God, or it would turn away from its Source-and-End, until at last it was withdrawn to the divine-minus its awareness of all it had learned, leaving both creation and the Creator poorer by its betrayal of its destiny."[216]

---

[215] *The Complete Edgar Cayce Readings*, Document #45026, 3744-002, (10/9/23), Q. 16 & Q. 22.
[216] Bro, *Begin a New Life*, 72.

16. *The Urantia Book* speaks of 'Gods', in a plural sense. The Cayce readings speak of 'Gods' and 'Gods of the universe.'[217] One reading states, "Hence those that speak of the Gods of the Universe are proper in their concept."[218]

17. *The Urantia Book* and the Cayce readings both depict the Book of Life as automatic libraries of divine records of truth, imprinted upon the substance of the universe, recording all intelligence of time for all eternity.[219]

18. The Cayce readings state that free will is sovereign, as does *The Urantia Book*.[220]

19. *The Urantia Book* and the Cayce readings both use the term *circuit*. *The Urantia Book* states that our "ascension is a part of the circuit of the seven superuniverses."[221] The Cayce readings refer to the Reincarnation Circuit as the way to ascend to the Father.[222]

20. Both the Cayce readings and *The Urantia Book* make use of the phrase, "the morning stars sang together." *The Urantia*

---

[217] *The Complete Edgar Cayce Readings*, Document #3842, 0254-017 Text, Q. 13, (12/11/24).
The Complete Edgar Cayce Readings, Document #45034, 3744-004 Text, Q. 40 & 41, (2/14/24).
The Complete Edgar Cayce Readings, Document #7862, 0294-007, (10/20/23).
The Complete Edgar Cayce Readings, Document #8778, 0301-003 Text, #7, (12/4/30).
[218] *The Complete Edgar Cayce Readings*, Document #9406, 0311-002 Text, Q. 6, (2/21/31).
[219] *The Urantia Book*, 301.
[220] *The Urantia Book*, 71, 615, 753.
[221] *The Urantia Book*, 63.
[222] *The Complete Edgar Cayce Readings*, Document #30642, 1602-003 Text, (9/22/39).

Book refers to these as conclaves of divine personalities.[223]
The Cayce readings also use this term to refer to such gatherings.[224]

21. Information, which came through the sleeping subject, depicted the earth as an experimental life world.[225] In *The Origin and Destiny of Man*, based on the Cayce readings, "the earth represents the third dimension testing laboratory for the entire system."[226]

22. *The Urantia Book* uses the term "seven psychic circles" to illustrate the progressive stages of spiritual development.[227] The Cayce readings refer to "man, in all his seven stages of development."[228]

23. One of the main themes of information which came through the sleeping subject was the Fatherhood of God and the brotherhood of man, mentioned specifically in at least 18 of the 196 Urantia Papers. The same terms are included together in at least 17 of Cayce's readings. For example, one of the readings states: "Raise not democracy or any other name above the Fatherhood of God and brotherhood of man."[229]

---

[223] *Urantia Book*, 87.
[224] *The Complete Edgar Cayce Readings*, Documents #56694, 37143, 32986, 11312, 11298, 10558, 8658, 7867.
[225] *Urantia Book*, 565.
[226] Lytle Robinson, *Edgar Cayce's Story of the Origin and Destiny of Man* (New York: Coward, McCann & Geoghegan, Inc., 1972) 33.
[227] *The Urantia Book*, 1209.
[228] *The Complete Edgar Cayce Readings*, Document #7320, 0281-025 Text, (7/17/35).
[229] *The Complete Edgar Cayce Readings*, Document #46594, 3976-024 Text, (6/16/39).

24. The authorship of the Gospels is described in *The Urantia Book* and the Cayce readings as follows:

The Urantia Book: The Gospel by Mark ... his record is in reality the Gospel according to Simon Peter.[230]

Cayce: Mark was first dictated, greatly by Peter.[231]

The Urantia Book: The Gospel of John ... though John did not write it.[232]

Cayce: John was written by several, not by the John who was the Beloved.[233]

25. Harold Sherman, a member of Sadler's Forum, stated that there was a group effort of higher orders of universe personalities working to communicate through the sleeping subject. The Cayce sources continually referred to themselves as "we". [234]

26. As recorded in *The Urantia Book*, the Forces speaking through the sleeping subject commented on the League of Nations.[235] Cayce made two trips to the White House at President Wilson's invitation, to give trance counsel on the League of Nations.[236]

---

[230] *The Urantia Book,* 1341.
[231] *The Complete Edgar Cayce Readings*, Document #30618, 1598-002 Text, #19, (5/29/38).
[232] *The Urantia Book,* 1342.
[233] *The Complete Edgar Cayce Readings*, Document #30618, 1598-002 Text, #19, (5/29/38).
[234] Bro, *Begin a New Life,* 9 & 24.
[235] *The Urantia Book,* 1489.
[236] Bro, *Begin a New Life,* 16.

27. *The Urantia Book* draws from Christian and various non-Christian religions around the world.[237] The readings seemed to draw from non-Christian traditions of India, of Egypt, of Persia and elsewhere.[238]

28. *The Urantia Book* teaches spiritual growth through experiential reality and says that "wisdom ... can be secured only through experience."[239] The Cayce readings also stress growth through experience.[240]

29. *The Urantia Book* and the Cayce readings reveal similar information about the work of the creative forces.

> Creation on earth was a blend of matter with mind (however primitive, mind was there in the tropism's and reactions of microorganisms, and in the polarities and valences of chemicals); but the driving, evolving Force was superordinate to either matter or mind alone, and expressed itself through these.[241]

30. *The Urantia Book* stresses the value and necessity of living a life of "wholehearted and loving service in unselfish ministry to one's fellow creatures.[242] The Cayce readings continually stress that the greater gain comes from service to others, and that our prayer should be for opportunities to serve as a blessing in other people's lives.[243]

[237] *The Urantia Book*, 1012, and general philosophical and religious content.
[238] Bro, *Begin a New Life*, 46.
[239] *The Urantia Book*, 907.
[240] Bro, *Begin a New Life*, 75.
[241] Bro, *Edgar Cayce on Religion and Psychic Experience*, 33.
[242] *The Urantia Book*, (p. 1000, for example) -- This is a significant theme within the text.
[243] *The Complete Edgar Cayce Readings*, Documents #56442, 48346, and 47682 are examples of this theme, which permeates the readings.

31. *The Urantia Book* says that "all of Jesus' followers sensed the impending crisis, but they were prevented from fully realizing its seriousness by the unusual cheerfulness and exceptional good humor of the Master."[244] The Cayce readings say that, as his final hours approached, Jesus was "merry -- even in the hour of trial. Joke[d] -- even in the hour of betrayal."[245]

32. Both *The Urantia Book* and Cayce identify Jesus as Michael.[246]

33. *The Urantia Book* teaches that souls from a given era on Earth incarnate as groups on the mansion worlds.[247] The Cayce readings teach that souls of a given era in general incarnate together.[248]

34. The following is a sentiment of both *The Urantia Book* and the Cayce readings:

> To build these two statements, that Christ was the Son of God and that he died for man's salvation, into a dogma, and then make salvation depend upon believing that dogma, has been a great psychological crime.[249]

---

[244] *Urantia Book*, 1880.
[245] *The Complete Edgar Cayce Readings*, Document #56914, 5749-001 Text, #6, (6/14/32).
[246] *The Complete Edgar Cayce Readings*, Document #3942, 0254-042 Text, (7/15/28).
[247] *Urantia Book*, 341-2.
[248] Cerminara, 43.
[249] Cerminara, 73.

35. Both *The Urantia Book*[250] and the Cayce readings identify John the Baptist and the prophet Samuel as members of the Nazarites.[251]

36. According to both Cayce and *The Urantia Book*, Jesus had a younger sister named Ruth, not mentioned by name in the Bible.

37. Both sources describe the rapid decomposition of the mortal remains of Jesus in the tomb. *The Urantia Book* states that "the dissolution of the mortal remains of Jesus of Nazareth was well-nigh instantaneous. When Mary Magdalene entered his tomb, she saw only the folded napkin where his head had rested and the bandages wherewith he had been wrapped lying intact and as they had rested on the stone before the celestial hosts removed the body."[252] Cayce said, "with the disintegration of the body, as indicated in the manner in which the shroud, the napkin lay, there was then the taking of the body-physical form."[253]

---

[250] *The Urantia Book*, 1496.
[251] *The Complete Edgar Cayce Readings*, Document #4210,254-109 Text, #9.
The Complete Edgar Cayce Readings, Document #56942,5749-8 Text, #3
The Complete Edgar Cayce Readings, Document #43102, 3344-2 Text, #5.
[252] *Urantia Book*, 2922, 2024.
[253] Anne Read, *Edgar Cayce on Jesus and His Church.* (New York: Paperback Library, 1970), 142.

Closing Statement

You have been presented with all of the information currently available in support of my thesis. There are some unanswered and perhaps unanswerable questions in regards to the foregoing information. Nevertheless, thinking individuals should endeavor to persevere in the quest for knowledge and truth. These are the keys to understanding and to mental and spiritual growth. Abraham Lincoln once said, "When a man ceases to grow, he dies."

This book is for those courageous individuals, who engage in the confrontation and consideration of new ideas, they who possess a sincere desire to grow. They are the individuals who give to mankind the assurance that knowledge will avoid the stagnation of complacency, because truth is ever unfolding.

I hope that the information in this book has helped you in some way.

Part V: Appendices

APPENDIX A

Appendix A: Dr. Sadler's Papers

The *History of the Urantia Movement* is a group of papers attributed to the authorship of Dr. Sadler, and appear in their entirety in this chapter.

***

HISTORY OF THE URANTIA MOVEMENT

Several members of this group who participated in the preliminary "contacts" which led up to the appearance of the Urantia Papers, had considerable experience in the investigation of psychic phenomena. This group early arrived at the conclusion that the phenomena connected with the personality, who was later associated with the Urantia Papers, was in no way similar to any other well-known type of psychic performance -- such as hypnotism, automatic writing, clairvoyance, trances, spirit mediumship, telepathy, or double personality.

It should be made clear that the antecedents of the Urantia Papers were in no way associated with so-called spiritualism -- with its seances and supposed communication with the spirits of departed human beings.

CONTACT ACTIVITIES PRECEDING THE URANTIA PAPERS

It would seem that, during these early years, our unseen friends were engaged in a thoroughgoing testing of the contact personality, rehearsing the technique of communication, selecting the Contact Commissioners -- in fact, in a general way -- setting the stage for the subsequent initiation of the presentation of the "Urantia Papers."

APPENDIX A

During these early years we were introduced to many new and, to us, somewhat strange concepts of the universe of universes and as concerned man and his life on earth.

Among these numerous new ideas of cosmology and philosophy, the following may be mentioned:

1. New concept of a far-flung cosmos

2. Millions of other inhabited worlds.

3. Introduction to scores of different and varied echelons of celestial personalities.

4. Confirmation of evolutionary origin of humankind -- even of an evolutionary cosmos.

5. Intimation of multiple Creator Deities.

6. Tentative testing of our theologic concepts. Patient determination of how far we might possibly go in the direction of modifying our theologic beliefs and philosophical opinions.

7. Without realizing it, over a period of twenty years, our fundamental religious views and attitudes had been considerably changed.

8. We had been familiarized with such terms as The First Source and Center, Havona, superuniverses, and the Supreme Being -- but we had but meager ideas as to the real meaning of these names.

9. We also heard such words as Master Spirits, outer space, and Power Directors. But, again, we understood little as to their meaning. We also learned about numerous orders of angels.

10. We heard about Thought Adjusters, but our concept of the meaning of the term was vague and indefinite.

11. We had acquired a fuzzy concept of the morontia level of existence -- but we never heard the word morontia used until the Papers started.

12. The midwayers were very real to us -- we frequently talked with them during our varied "contacts." We quite fully understood that the secondary midwayers supervised the contacts.

13. We heard some things about the Lucifer rebellion, but got little information about Adam and Eve.

14. We gained the impression that there were special reasons for Jesus' bestowal on Urantia, but we had little or no idea as to the nature of these unrevealed reasons.

15. We listened to occasional references to Jesus' life and teachings -- but they were very cautious about the introduction of any new concepts regarding Michael's Urantia bestowal. Of all the Urantia Revelation the Jesus Papers were the biggest surprise.

16. While we did not hear the term "Corps of the Finality," we did pick up a hazy idea that Paradise might be the destination of surviving mortals.

Our superhuman friends thus spent upward of two decades in extending our cosmic horizons, enlarging our theologic concepts, and expanding our over-all philosophy.

We never realized how our religious thinking had been expanded until the Papers began to arrive. As the Revelation progressed we came more fully to appreciate how we had been prepared for the vast alteration of our religious beliefs by these preliminary contacts extending over a period of twenty years of pre-education.

Our apprenticeship training for subsequent service in association with the presentation of the Urantia Papers was facilitated by the fact that, except for contacts with the midwayers, no two contacts were alike. Seldom did we meet the visiting personalities more than once.

170

APPENDIX A

Every contact was entirely different from any and all that had gone before. And all of this experience was an extensive and liberal preparatory educational training in the expansion of our cosmology, theology, and philosophy -- not to mention our introduction to new ideas and concepts concerning a vast array of more mundane subjects.

The limited discussion of Jesus' life and teachings during these pre-revelatory contacts might be explained by the fact that the midwayers were a bit dubious as to how much authority they had in such matters -- as shown later on when a whole year was consumed in the clarification of their right to retell the story of the Michael bestowal.

Those of us who early attended upon these nocturnal vigils never suspected that we were in contact with anything supernatural.

During these early years, all of our observations and investigations utterly failed to reveal the psychic technique of reducing messages to writing.

HOW THE URANTIA PAPERS STARTED

After about twenty years of contact experience, an alleged student-visitor, speaking through this sleeping subject during one of these nocturnal vigils, in answer to one of our questions, said: "If you only knew what you are in contact with you would not ask such trivial questions. You would rather ask such questions as might elicit answers of supreme value to the human race."

This was something of a shock, as well as a mild rebuke, and caused all of us to look upon this unique experience in a new and different way. Later on that night, one of our number said: "Now they have asked for it -- let us give them questions that no human being can answer."

Now it is best to let matters rest here while we shift this narrative to a new and different setting.

HOW THE FORUM STARTED

Dr. William S. Sadler, a member of this early group of observers and investigators, tells the following story regarding the origin of that group of interested individuals which later on became known as the "Forum." He says: "On my way to the University of Kansas to deliver some lectures on Gestalt psychology, I wrote a letter to my son, age 16, saying that I thought doctors should try to maintain some contact with their old patients. I suggested that he talk with his mother about the feasibility of inviting some of our old friends to meet with us on Sunday afternoons for an hour or two of informal discussion and social exchange.

"When I returned to Chicago one Sunday morning I found that my wife had invited a group of our old patients to meet at our house that afternoon at three o'clock. It was the plan to conduct these Sunday afternoon gatherings somewhat as follows: First have a talk on some health topic -- such as the treatment of common colds, the cause and cure of worry, and then, after a cup of tea, engage in informal discussions -- asking and answering questions.

"As time passed, this group became a cosmopolitan gathering consisting of professional men and women -- doctors, lawyers, dentists, ministers, teachers -- together with individuals from all walks of life, farmers housewives, secretaries, office workers, and common laborers."

INTRODUCTION OF THE FORUM TO THE "CONTACTS"

The doctor continues his narrative: "Presently, I was asked to give a series of talks on "Mental Hygiene," or "Psychic Phenomena." At the beginning of my first talk, I said: "With one or two exceptions, all of the psychic phenomena which I have investigated have turned out to be either conscious or unconscious frauds. Some were deliberate frauds -- others were those peculiar cases in which the performer was a victim of the deceptions of his own subconscious mind."

APPENDIX A

"I had no more than said this, when one of the group spoke up, saying: "Doctor, if you have contacted something which you have been unable to solve -- it would be interesting -- tell us more about it."

"I asked Dr. Lena to get some notes she had taken at a recent "contact" and read them to the group. It should be understood that up to this time there was no secrecy connected with this case. The Urantia Papers had not begun to appear.

"It was at about this time that this group meeting at our house on Sunday afternoons began to be called the "Forum."

"The group manifested such a great interest in this case that I never did get around to giving any of the health talks such as had been planned.

"It was while these informal discussion were going on from week to week that the challenge came to us suggesting that if we would ask more serious questions we might get information of value to all mankind."

THE FORUM BEGINS TO ASK QUESTIONS

"We told the Forum all about this and invited them to join us in the preparation of questions. We decided to start out with questions pertaining to the origin of the cosmos, Deity, creation, and such other subjects as were far beyond the present-day knowledge of all humankind.

"The following Sunday several hundred questions were brought in. We sorted out these questions, discarding duplicates, and in a general way, classifying them. Shortly thereafter, the first Urantia Paper appeared in answer to these questions. From first to last, when the Papers appeared, the questions disappeared.

"This was the procedure followed throughout the many years of the reception of the Urantia Papers. No questions -- no papers."

THE FORUM BECOMES A CLOSED GROUP

About this time, the Forum, as it were, was taken away from us. We were instructed to form a "closed group" -- requiring each member to sign a pledge of secrecy and to discuss the Papers and all matters pertaining thereto with only those persons who were members of the Forum.

Membership tickets were issued and the Charter membership numbered Thirty. The date of this organization was September, 1925. Seventeen of these Charter members are still living.

The individuals charged with the responsibility of gathering up the questions and comparing the typewritten text with the original handwritten manuscript, came to be known as the "Contact Commissioners." From that date forward only these Contact Commissioners attended "Contacts" and received written communications through the contact personality.

From time to time new members were received into the Forum, after being interviewed by the officers and after signing the same pledge that was signed by the original Charter Members. This pledge read: "We acknowledge our pledge of secrecy, renewing our promise not to discuss the Urantia Revelations or their subject matter with any one save active Forum members, and to take no notes of such matter as is read or discussed at the public sessions, or make copies or notes of what we personally read."

The last meeting of the Forum as a genetic assembly was held on May 31st, 1942. During the 17 years of official existence the Forum attained a total membership of 486. From this date in 1942 the Forum continued as a study group to the time of the organization of the First Urantia Society.

During the period of the reception of the Urantia Papers upward of 300 different persons participated in asking these genetic questions. With but a few exceptions, all of the Urantia Papers were given in response to such questions.

APPENDIX A

THE FIRST URANTIA PAPERS

The first group of Papers numbered 57. We then received a communication suggesting that since we could now ask many and much more intelligent questions, the superhuman agencies and personalities responsible for transmitting the 57 Papers would engage to enlarge the revelation and to expand the Papers in accordance with our new questions.

This was the plan: We would read a Paper on Sunday afternoon and the following Sunday the new questions would be presented. Again, these would be sorted, classified, etc. This program covered several years and ultimately resulted in the presentation of the 196 Papers as now found in *The Urantia Book*.

RECEIVING THE COMPLETED PAPERS

In a way, there was a third presentation. After receiving these 196 Papers, we were told that the "Revelatory Commission" would be pleased to have us go over the Papers once more and ask questions concerning the "Clarification of Concepts" and the "Removal of Ambiguities." This program again covered several years. During this period very little new information was imparted. Only minor changes were made in any of the Papers. Some matter was added -- some removed -- but there was little revision or amplification of the text.

What has just been recorded refers more particularly to Parts I, II, and III of *The Urantia Book*. Part IV -- The Jesus Papers -- had a little different origin. They were produced by a midwayer commission and were completed one year later than the other Papers. The first three parts were completed and certified to us in AD. 1934. The Jesus Papers were not so delivered to us until 1935.

THE DELAY IN RECEIVING THE JESUS PAPERS

The delay of one year in the reception of the Jesus Papers -- Part IV of *The Urantia Book* -- may be explained as follows: The midwayers were a bit apprehensive about becoming involved in the suit pending in the universe courts -- Gabriel vs. Lucifer -- and they hesitated to complete their project until they were assured that they had full authority to retell the story of Jesus' life on earth.

After some months' waiting there came the mandate from Uversa directing the United Midwayers of Urantia to proceed with their project of revealing the story of the life and teachings of Michael when incarnated on Urantia, and not only assuring them that they were not in "contempt" of the Uversa courts, but instead granting them a mandate to do this service and admonishing any and all persons connected therewith to refrain from interfering with, or in any way hindering, the execution of such an undertaking.

And this is the explanation of why the Jesus Papers appear one year after the other Papers had been completed.

REASON FOR SILENCE RESPECTING DETAILS OF THE ORIGIN OF *THE URANTIA BOOK*

Among the several reasons given us at the time we were requested not to discuss the details of our personal experiences associated with the origin of *The Urantia Book*, the two major reasons were the following:

1. Unknown Features. There is much connected with the appearance of the Urantia Papers which no human being fully understands. None of us really knows just how this phenomenon was executed. There are numerous missing links in our understanding of how this revelation came to appear in written English.

    If any one of us should tell any one <u>all</u> he really knows about the technique and methods employed throughout the years of our getting this Revelation, such a narration would satisfy no one -- there are too many missing links.

APPENDIX A

2. The main reason for not revealing the identity of the "Contact Personality" is that the Celestial Revelators do not want any human being -- any human name -- ever to be associated with *The Urantia Book.* They want this revelation to stand on its own declarations and teachings.

    They are determined that future generations shall have the book wholly free from all mortal connections -- they do not want a Saint Peter, Saint Paul, Luther, Calvin, or Wesley. The book does not even bear the imprint of the printer who brought the book into being.

    Remember: You could appreciate a good poem -- even if you did not know the author. Likewise, you could enjoy a symphony even if you were ignorant of the composer.

HOW WE GOT THE URANTIA PAPERS

Just about all that is known or could be told about the origin of the Urantia Papers is to be found, here and there, in *The Urantia Book.* A list of such references is to be found on the back of the dust jacket of the Book.

Let us take a brief look at these citations.

1. Page 1, par. 2. This passage refers to the difficulty of presenting expanded spiritual concepts when restricted to circumscribed human language, such as English.

2. Page 1, par. 4. An Orvonton Commission participated in the revelation and prepared this Foreword.

3. Page 17, par. 1. In presenting this revelation of augmented spiritual values and universe meanings, more than one thousand human concepts were drawn from the minds of human beings of the present and the past.

4. Page 16, par. 8. P.1343, par. 1. In all revelation of truth, preference is given to the highest existing human concepts of ideality

and reality. Only in the absence of the human concept is super-human knowledge revealed.

5. Page 1109, par. 4. Revelators are seldom at liberty to anticipate scientific discoveries. Truth is timeless, but the teachings respecting the physical sciences and certain phases of cosmology will become partially obsolescent as the result of the new discoveries of advancing scientific investigations. The cosmology of the Urantia Revelation is not inspired. Human wisdom must evolve.

6. Page 215, par. 2-9. Human pedagogy proceeds from the simple to the complex. The Urantia Revelation begins with the more complex and goes on the consideration of the more simple. Instead of beginning with man reaching up for God, the Urantia Papers begin with God -- reaching down and finding man.

7. Page 865. par. 6-7. The narrative of the midwayers function in initiating and carrying forward to completion the Urantia Revelation.

8. Page 865, par. 2, P.1208, par. 7. Midway creatures are always employed in the phenomena of communication with material beings through the technique of "Contact Personalities." The "subject" through whom the Urantia Papers were bestowed had a highly experienced Thought Adjuster. The "subject's" relative indifference and unconcern regarding the work of his indwelling Adjuster was in every way favorable to the execution and completion of this revelatory project.

9. Page 1256, par. 1. The contact personality was a member of the Urantia Reserve Corps of Destiny. This was just one of several conditions favoring the impartation of the Urantia Revelation.

10. Page 1003, par. 3. The Urantia Revelation is unique in that it is presented by multiple authors. The Urantia Revelation, like its predecessors, is not inspired.

11. Page 32, par. 2. A Divine Counselor "portrays the reality and nature of the Father with unchallengeable authority."

APPENDIX A

12. Page 17, par. 2. The Revelators depend upon the indwelling Adjusters and the Spirit of Truth to help us in the appropriation of the truth in the Urantia Revelation.

13. Page 1007, par. 1. Revelation keeps us in touch with evolution. Revelation is adapted to the age of its bestowal. New revelation maintains contact with preceding revelations.

HOW WE DID NOT GET *THE URANTIA BOOK*

Recently, a group of ministers from northern Indiana, who were engaged in studying *The Urantia Book,* spent the day with us and, during the evening, Dr., Sadler led a discussion on "How We Did Not Get *The Urantia Book.*"

The following is a gist of that presentation:

PSYCHIC PHENOMENA

UNUSUAL ACTIVITIES OF THE MARGINAL CONSCIOUSNESS
(The Subconscious Mind)
1. Automatic Writing.
2. Automatic talking.
   a. Speaking with "Tongues."
   b. Trance Mediums.
   c. Spirit Mediums.
   d. Catalepsy.
3. Automatic Hearing. -- Clairaudience.
   Hearing "Voices."
4. Automatic Seeing.
   a. Dream States -- Twilight Mentation.
   b. Visions -- Automatic Dramatization.
   c. Hallucinations. (Shifty "Reality" Feelings.)
5. Automatic Thinking.
   a. Automatic Fearing -- Anxiety Neurosis.
   b. Automatic Ideation -- Mental Compulsions.
   c. Automatic Judgments -- Intuition, "Hunches."
   d. Automatic Association of Ideas -- Premonitions.
   e. Automatic Guessing -- E.S.P., Extra-Sensory Perception.
   f. Automatic Deductions -- Delusions, Paranoia.
   g. Dominance by Marginal Consciousness -- Dreams and
      Hypnosis.
6. Automatic Remembering.
   a. Clairvoyance -- Automatic Memory Associations.
   b. Telepathy -- Mind Reading (?).
   c. Fortune Telling (Largely Fraudulent.)
   d. Musical and Mathematical Marvels.

APPENDIX A

7. <u>Automatic Acting.</u>
    a. Automatic Behavior -- (Major Hysteria, Witchcraft.)
    b. Automatic motion -- Motor compulsions.
    c. Automatic Overdrives -- Manic Episodes.
    d. Automatic Walking -- Somnambulism.
8. <u>Automatic personalization.</u>
    a. Automatic forgetting -- Amnesia.
    b. Automatic Dissociation -- Double and Multiple Personality.
    c. Schizophrenia -- Split Personality.
9. <u>Combined and Associated Psychic States.</u>

<u>Note</u>: The technique of the reception of *The Urantia Book* in English in no way parallels or impinges upon any of the above phenomena of the marginal consciousness.

FUNCTIONING OF THE CONTACT COMMISSIONERS

During these early years the Contact Commissioners received many communications and directives in writing. Almost all of these messages had a notation at the bottom of the last page which read: "To be destroyed by fire not later than the appearance of the Urantia Papers in print." It was the design of our unseen friends to prevent the appearance of an "Urantia Apocrypha" subsequent to the publication of *The Urantia Book*.

All of this was encouraging to us in that it assured us that the Urantia Papers would some time be published. It sustained our hopes throughout the long waiting years of delay.

The fact that no provision was ever made for replacing members of the Contact Commission who might be lost through disability or death, also led us to entertain the belief that the Book would be published during the lifetime of some of us.

The Commissioners were the custodians of the Urantia manuscript, keeping the carbon copy of the typewritten transcript in a fireproof vault. They were also charged with full responsibility for supervising all the details connected with the publication of the Book, securing the international copyrights, etc.

We were enjoined to refrain from discussing the identity of the Contact Personality and, after the publication of the Book, to make no statement at any time as to whether the "subject" was still living or was deceased.

THE SEVENTY

In 1939, some of us thought the time had come when we should form a class to engage in the more serious and systematic study of the Urantia Papers. This project was presented to the Forum and when those who wished to join such a group were counted, it was found that just 70 persons desired to enter upon this study. So for several years this class was referred to as "The Seventy." Two or three years preceding the formation of The Seventy an informal group had been meeting on Wednesday evenings.

The Seventy carried on systematic study of the Urantia Papers from April 3, 1939 to the summer of 1956, and was the forerunner of the later "School of the Urantia Brotherhood."

During these years the Seventy enrolled 107 students.

The Seventy carried on its work of study, thesis writing, and practice of teaching for 17 years. During this period eight written communications were given to the Seventy by the Seraphim of Progress attached to the Superhuman Planetary Government of Urantia.

THE PUBLICATION MANDATE

At long last, permission to publish the Urantia Papers was granted. The Introduction to this mandate reads:

"We regard *The Urantia Book* as a feature of the progressive evolution of human society. It is not germane to the spectacular episode of epochal revelation, even though it may apparently be timed to appear in the wake of one such revelation in human society. The Book belongs to the era immediately to follow the conclusion of the present ideological struggle. That will be the day when men will be willing to seek truth and righteousness. When the chaos of the present confusion has passed, it will be more readily possible to formulate the cosmos of a new and improved era of human relationships. And it is for this better order of affairs on earth that the book has been made ready.

"But the publication of the book has not been postponed to that (possibly) somewhat remote date. An early publication of the book has been provided so that it may be in hand for the training of leaders and teachers. Its presence is also required to engage the attention of persons of means who may be thus led to provide funds for translation into other languages."

Upon receipt of these instructions, the Contact Commissioners entered upon the task of publishing *The Urantia Book* and preparation of plans for its distribution.

The Papers were published just as we received them. The Contact Commissioners had no editorial authority. Our job was limited to "spelling, capitalization, and punctuation."

Before the demise of Dr. Lena K. Sadler in August, 1939 she had collected about twenty thousand dollars for the publication fund, and this was used to set type and prepare plates for the printing of the Book.

THE URANTIA FOUNDATION

It was those plates of *The Urantia Book* which constituted the basis for the formation of the Urantia Foundation. This Foundation, set up under the laws of Illinois, was completed on January 11, 1950. The first Board of Trustees were: William N. Hales, President; William S. Sadler, Jr., Vice President; Emma L. Christensen, Secretary; Wilfred C. Kellogg, Treasurer; and Edith Cook, Assistant Secretary.

It was learned that one of the wealthy members of the Forum desired to contribute fifty thousand dollars for the publication of the Book. By instruction, this was circumvented, because, they told us, it was best to give all parties concerned an opportunity to contribute to the publication fund.

Accordingly, an appeal was made for $50,000.00 to defray the expenses of printing ten thousand copies. The response was immediate. The sum contributed was in excess of forty-nine thousand dollars. The first money to reach the Foundation office was one thousand dollars from the late Sir Hubert Wilkins, the Arctic explorer.

The Book was published under international copyright October 12, 1955.

THE URANTIA BROTHERHOOD

It was inevitable that some sort of fraternal organization would grow out of the teachings of *The Urantia Book*. All interested persons could see that the Urantia teachings were opposed to the sectarianism of Christian believers. It was clear that it was not the purpose of the Urantia Revelation to start a new church.

Accordingly, on January 2, 1955, a group of persons who believed the teachings of the Book and who were interested in their proclamation, assembled in Chicago and completed the organization of the Urantia Brotherhood, a voluntary and fraternal organization of Urantia believers. This group composed the charter membership of the Urantia Brotherhood, and was 36 in number.

A Constitution and By-laws were adopted, and since that date numerous Societies have been formed throughout the United States.

When ten or more persons who are familiar with, and believe in, the teachings of *The Urantia Book* so desire they may be chartered as a Urantia Society. Membership in any church or fraternal organization does not interfere with becoming a member of a Urantia Society.

The original organizers of the Brotherhood and their successors were to direct the organization for the first nine years. Thereafter, the

APPENDIX A

Brotherhood would be ordered by the action of a Triennial Delegate Assembly composed of delegates from the various Urantia Societies.

The Departmental Committees of the Brotherhood are:

Judicial Committee
Charter Committee
Fraternal Relations Committee
Domestic Relations Committee
Foreign Extension Committee
Committee on Education
Publication Committee
Finance Committee
Committee on Miscellaneous Activities

The Chairmen of the Committees, together with the Brotherhood officers, constitute the Executive Committee of the Brotherhood.

The all-over purpose of the Brotherhood is well expressed in the Preamble to the Constitution.

PREAMBLE

"Inasmuch as it is our most solemn conviction that the comfort, happiness, and well-being of man will be enhanced by the creation of an organization devoted to the purposes hereinafter expressed may best be accomplished through the mutual assistance and association of a body of people working together for a common cause, we do hereby unite together as a voluntary association and fellowship under the name of Urantia Brotherhood, and we do hereby adopt and establish this Constitution of Urantia Brotherhood."

The original 56 Founders became the General Council which was designed to govern the Brotherhood for its first nine years.

The First Urantia Society of Chicago was organized and granted Charter No. 1 on June 17, 1956. The Society had 34 Charter Members. The present membership of the First Society is 142.

ACTIVITIES OF URANTIA BROTHERHOOD

In cooperation with the Urantia Foundation, the Brotherhood is just now interested in the completion of the Index to *The Urantia Book* -- in reality, a concordance. Its publication is hoped for in 1961.

We are all interested in the progress of a French translation which is in final review and may be published late in 1961 or early in 1962.

The Brotherhood recently completed the formulation of a "Funeral Service" consisting of Scriptural passages and appropriate selections from *The Urantia Book.*

The Brotherhood sponsors a Quarterly News Letter which the Executive Committee sends to all Urantia Societies and other interested persons.

The Brotherhood fosters many study groups scattered throughout the United States and in foreign countries. Eventually, most of these study groups will develop into Urantia Societies.

During the last year two Field Representatives have been appointed to foster the individual Urantia Societies and pay them visits periodically.

In December, 1959, the Internal Revenue Bureau of the United States government ruled that the Urantia Foundation, the Urantia Brotherhood, and the Urantia Brotherhood Corporation were exempt from paying income taxes, and that any and all contributions made to these organizations are deductible from the income tax of such donors.

The Van Award, Section Three of Article Thirteen of the Constitution of the Urantia Brotherhood reads: "If in the opinion of the Executive Committee, any member of Urantia Brotherhood shall perform or render some unusual, extraordinary, or distinguished service, the Executive Committee shall present to the General Council the name of such member with the recommendation that a suitable award or citation in recognition thereof be given. Upon the presentation of such recommendation, the General Council, by unanimous vote of all Councilors present at any duly constituted meeting, may give or confer on such member such award or citation in recognition of the unusual, extraordinary, or distinguished service of such member as the General Council may deem fitting and appropriate."

On January 25, 1959, the first award under this Constitutional provision was made to the President of the Urantia Brotherhood School.

The reason for denominating this "The Van Award" is recited in the declaration of the award, and reads as follows:

> "The spiritual insight and moral steadfastness which
> enabled Van to maintain such an unshakable attitude of
> loyalty to the universe government was the product of
> clear thinking, wise reasoning, logical judgment,
> sincere motivation, unselfish purpose, intelligent
> loyalty, experiential memory, disciplined character, and
> the unquestioning dedication of his personality to the
> doing of the will of the Father in Paradise."

The conclusion of the award says: "in honor of his many years of devoted and distinguished service in behalf of the Urantia movement."

DISTRIBUTION OF THE URANTIA BOOK

At the time of the publication of *The Urantia Book* we were given many suggestions respecting the methods we should employ in the work of its distribution. These instructions may be summarized as follows:

1. Study the methods employed by Jesus in introducing his work on the earth. Note how quietly he worked at first -- so often after even a miracle, he would admonish the recipient of his ministry, saying: "Tell no man what has happened to you."

2. We were advised to avoid all efforts to achieve early and spectacular recognition.

3. During the first five years, these methods have been adhered to. The distribution increases yearly. At present, more than fifty book stores, from coast to coast, carry the Book.

The vast majority of the Brotherhood have concurred in this sort of quiet and gradual presentation of the Book. Only a few individuals have exhibited some restlessness and craving for aggressive plans for increased distribution.

One thing should be made clear: Nothing is done to interfere with the energetic and enthusiastic efforts of any individual to introduce *The Urantia Book* to his varied contacts and human associations.

URANTIA BROTHERHOOD CORPORATION

Since the Urantia Brotherhood is not a corporation -- a legal entity -- the Urantia Brotherhood Corporation was formed under the laws of the State of Illinois, designed to provide for corporations not for profit, to serve as the legal arm of the fraternal and voluntary association of the Urantia Brotherhood.

This Corporation is the fiscal agent of the Brotherhood and in a general way takes care of the varied financial and legal interests of the Brotherhood.

THE URANTIA BROTHERHOOD SCHOOL

Among the early activities of the Brotherhood was the organization of the School of the Brotherhood which began its first session in September, 1956. The degree granted after three years of training is that of "Ordained Teacher." A shorter course of study leads to the status of "Certified Leader."

The School is conducted by the Educational Committee. Many textbooks have been prepared for use in the School and for use by a future Correspondence School which will no doubt materialize as *The Urantia Book* continues to be distributed throughout the world.

APPENDIX A

The following textbooks have been prepared:

The Theology of *The Urantia Book*, Part I.
The Theology of *The Urantia Book*, Part II.
The Theology of *The Urantia Book*, Part III.
The Theology of *The Urantia Book*, Part IV.
The Teachings of Jesus.
The Short Course in Doctrine.
Worship and Wisdom.
Science in *The Urantia Book*, Vol. I.
Science in *The Urantia Book*, Vol. II.
Topical Studies, Vol. I.
Topical Studies, Vol. II.

In Preparation

The Urantia Book and the New Testament.
Analytic Studies in Part I.
Analytic Studies in Part II.
Diagrams and Maps.

The course of study is planned to cover a three years' seminary education. At present, only part time work is provided at evening sessions.

The curriculum embraces courses in the following subjects:

Techniques of public speaking
Leadership and Teaching
Comparative Religion
Educational Psychology
Christian Sects and Denominations
Homiletics
Old and New Testament History
Presentation of *The Urantia Book*
Studies in *The Urantia Book*:
    Urantia Doctrine
    Synthetic Studies
    Topical Studies
    Life of Christ

Worship and Wisdom
Short Course in Doctrine
Comparison with the Four Gospels
Science in *The Urantia Book*
Critical Analyses

As yet, no degrees of "Ordained Teacher" have been granted, but diplomas as "Certified Leader" have been given to 14 individuals.

The number of registered students taking credit courses has averaged about thirty. A like number of "auditors" attend the classes.

(This ends the word for word reproduction of Dr. Sadler's papers.)

Appendix B: Dr. William S. Sadler

Following is information concerning Dr. Sadler from *The National Cyclopaedia of American Biography*: Volume 54, p. 418:

SADLER, William Samuel, psychiatrist, was born in Spencer, Ind., June 24, 1875, son of Samuel Cavins and Sarah Isabella (Wilson) Sadler, grandson of William Cavins and Mary (Wharton) Sadler, and great-grandson of John Madison and Frances (Chisholm) Sadler. His father was a salesman and musician. William S. Sadler received his preliminary education from private tutors, attended Battle Creek (Mich.) College for a time, studied at Cooper Medical College (later part of Stanford University) San Francisco, CA., during 1901-03, and was *graduated MD in 1906* at the American Medical Missionary College, Chicago Ill. In 1910 he engaged in the study of psychiatry at clinics in Leeds, England, and in Vienna, Austria, where he attended classed conducted by Sigmund Freud and Alfred Adler. In the meantime, while attending Battle Creek College he worked at Battle Creek Sanitarium. In 1895 he went to Chicago, where he was employed as secretary of the Chicago Medical Missions, an undertaking which operated a dozen or more social service enterprises and at that time was one of the large private charities. He continued as secretary until 1901. Upon graduating at medical college, he established a private practice in Chicago, specializing in surgery until 1930 when he began specializing in psychiatry, carrying on in that field until a year before his death. In addition to his private practice, he was on the staff of Columbus Hospital, Chicago, from 1918 to 1929, after which he was consulting psychiatrist there until 1940. Furthermore, he was director *of the Chicago Institute of Research and Diagnosis* during his years of practice, and served as psychiatric consultant and a *trustee of the Q.K. Kellogg Foundation, Battle Creek, Mich.*, during 1937-39. In the area of education, Sadler was an instructor in surgery and related subjects at the Post Graduate Medical Center, Chicago, in 1905-06 and professor of pastoral psychiatry at McCormick Theological Seminary, Chicago, during 1930-57. As a he encouraged religious study by his patients. *He was the author of some forty books* on physical and mental hygiene, health, and other medical topics, including:

The Physiology of Faith and Fear, 1912, 9th ed. 1925
Race Decadence, 1922
The Truth About Heredity, 1927
Long Heads and Round Heads, 1918
The Mind at Mischief, 1929
The Elements of Pep, 1925
What a Salesman Should Know About His Health, 1923
Cause and Cure of Colds, (with his wife), 1930
The Theory and Practice of Psychiatry, 1936
The Sex Life, (with his wife), 1938
Prescription for Permanent Peace, 1944
Practice of Psychiatry, 1953

He also wrote numerous articles on health and psychiatry for professional and popular journals, the latter including *American Magazine* and *The Ladies Home Journal.* From 1908 to 1923 he lectured on the Chautauqua circuit. A life fellow of the American College of Surgeons and a fellow of the American Psychiatric Association, American Medical Association, and American Medical Association for the Advancement of Science, he was a member of the American Psycho pathological Association, Illinois Psychiatric Association. Illinois Society for Mental Hygiene, Chicago Society for Personality Study, Illinois State Medical Society, Chicago Medical Society, Gorgas Memorial Institute in Tropical and Preventive Medicine, National Association of Authors and Journalists, _Eugene Field Society of Chicago, and the International Mark Twain Society_. In politics he was a Republican. His special interests included writing, lecturing, golfing, fishing, and traveling. He was married in Paris, Ill., Dec. 3, 1897, to Lena Celestia, daughter of Smith Moses Kellogg of that place, a manufacturer, and had two sons: Willis Kellogg (died in infancy) and William Samuel; and a foster daughter, Christy. William S. Sadler died in Chicago, Ill. April 26, 1969.
[emphasis mine]

[end *National Cyclopaedia*]

Appendix C: Dates Cayce was in Chicago

Date	Doc. #	Notes from reading
1. 03/16/11	35356	I spent most of my time at the Institute [in Chicago]
2. 05/01/23	45766	Cayce in Chicago at Washington Hotel
3. 05/01/23	45102	Cayce in Chicago at Washington Hotel
4. 05/01/23	45896	Cayce in Chicago
5. 05/01/23	1146	Cayce in Chicago at LaSalle Hotel
6. 05/02/23	38970	Cayce in Chicago at Washington Hotel
7. 05/02/23	45862	Cayce in Chicago
8. 05/02/23	45890	Cayce in Chicago at Washington Hotel
9. 07/13/24	3808	Cayce in Chicago at Washington Hotel
10. 07/17/24	45650	Cayce in Chicago at Washington Hotel
11. 07/17/24	45654	Cayce in Chicago at Washington Hotel
12. 07/18/24	45658	Cayce in Chicago at Washington Hotel
13. 07/18/24	48799	Cayce in Chicago at Washington Hotel
14. 07/18/24	26363	Cayce in Chicago at Washington Hotel
15. 07/19/24	45662	Cayce in Chicago at Washington Hotel
16. 07/19/24	45990	Cayce in Chicago
17. 07/20/24	45178	Cayce in Chicago at Washington Hotel
18. 07/19/24	18722	Cayce in Chicago at Washington Hotel
19. 07/20/24	45666	Cayce in Chicago at Washington Hotel
20. 07/21/24	37562	Cayce in Chicago at Washington Hotel
21. 07/21/24	38974	Cayce in Chicago at Washington Hotel
22. 07/21/24	38978	Cayce in Chicago at Washington Hotel
23. 07/22/24	48830	Cayce in Chicago at Washington Hotel
24. 07/22/24	10374	Cayce in Chicago at Washington Hotel
25. 07/22/24	238	Cayce in Chicago at Washington Hotel
26. 07/24/24	38982	Cayce in Chicago at Washington Hotel
27 07/24/24	39918	Cayce in Chicago at Washington Hotel
28. 07/25/24	49878	Cayce in Chicago at Washington Hotel
29. 07/25/24	56722	Cayce in Chicago at Washington Hotel
30. 07/25/24	56794	Cayce in Chicago at Washington Hotel
31. 07/26/24	48798	Cayce in Chicago at Washington Hotel
32. 07/26/24	48800	Cayce in Chicago at Washington Hotel
33. 07/26/24	50438	Cayce in Chicago at Washington Hotel
34. 07/26/24	50602	Cayce in Chicago at Washington Hotel

Date	Doc. #	Notes from reading
35. 07/26/24	50604	Cayce in Chicago at Washington Hotel
36. 07/28/24	486	Cayce in Chicago at Washington Hotel
37. 07/29/24	45670	Cayce in Chicago at Washington Hotel
38. 07/29/24	50198	Cayce in Chicago at Washington Hotel
39. 07/29/24	23758	Cayce in Chicago at Washington Hotel
40. 07/30/24	3814	Cayce in Chicago at Washington Hotel
41. 07/30/24	6474	Cayce in Chicago at Washington Hotel
42. 10/05/24	51708	I have as many or more friends in Chicago as anywhere
43. 02/23/25	51752	While I was in Chicago
44. 04/05/27	51976	Cayce says he may be in Chicago a few days or a few weeks
45. 10/07/27	55988	Cayce planning Chicago trip in 30-60 days
46. 11/06/27	22226	Cayce instructed to go to Chicago
47. 11/14/27	51976	Cayce in Chicago 11/14/27-11/21-27
48. 11/14/27	51976	Cayce left for Chicago
49. 11/18/27	2658	Sister's apartment, Hotel Sheridan Plaza, Chicago
50. 02/28/28	47304	(letter date) May be going to Chicago next week
51. 03/07/28	56775	Cayce in Chicago at Washington Hotel from 3/7/28-3/11/28
52. 03/08/28	35794	Cayce in Chicago in LaSalle Hotel
53. 03/08/28	49806	Cayce in Chicago in LaSalle Hotel
54. 03/08/28	50350	Cayce in Chicago in LaSalle Hotel
55. 03/09/28	50354	Cayce in Chicago in LaSalle Hotel
56. 03/09/28	56442	Cayce in Chicago in LaSalle Hotel
57. 03/10/28	56434	Cayce in Chicago in LaSalle Hotel
58. 03/10/28	22318	Cayce in Chicago at LaSalle Hotel
59. 03/10/28	1538	Cayce in Chicago at LaSalle Hotel
60. 03/11/28	51102	Cayce in Chicago in LaSalle Hotel
61. 03/11/28	2682	Cayce in Chicago at LaSalle Hotel
62. 03/15/28	33420	Cayce just returned from Chicago
63. 03/16/28	46696	Cayce just returned from Chicago
64. 03/17/28	30832	(letter date) Was in Chicago for a week
65. 03/22/28	27520	Return from Chicago
66. 07/06/30	2686	Cayce to go to Chicago Nov. or Dec.
67. 10/10/31	35116	(letter date) planning winter trip to Chicago
68. 03/28/32	35116	(letter date) hoping to be in Chicago in the spring

Date	Doc. #	Notes from reading
69. 05/10/32	35348	summer or fall ... may be able to come to Chicago
70. 07/06/32	35348	(letter date) planning Chicago trip in summer or fall
71. 07/06/32	35348	planning Chicago trip early fall
72. 11/29/32	35356	Cayce always enjoyed his visits to the Institute in Chicago
73. 01/31/33	10772	(letter date) Chicago trip referred to
74. 02/16/33	47872	(letter date) Planning trip to Chicago in spring or summer
75. 02/21/33	35976	Hoping to come to Chicago in the spring
76. 07/16/34	16360	Planning 10 day to 2 week trip for October
77. 08/20/34	37440	Considering trip to Chicago
78. 11/11/34	18248	Chicago trip fell through
79. 06/22/37	33167	Cayce in Chicago January, 1936
80. 03/15/39	32624	Cayce in Chicago at Hotel Great Northern

Appendix D: Cayce-Urantia Timeline

C	Event
1830	♦The Kentucky Educational Society is formed[254]
1868	♦James Redpath forms Redpath Lyceum Chautauqua Bureau[255]
1874	♦First Chautauqua in the world held at Lake Chautauqua, NY[256]
1876	♦Sadler born Spencer, IN[257]
1877	♦Cayce born Mar. 10 on farm near Hopkinsville, KY[258]
1888	♦James Redpath visits Jefferson Davis in Kentucky for 3 months[259]
1889	♦Sadler moves to Battle Creek[260]
1891	♦Sadler in Fort Wayne, IN[261]
	♦James Redpath dies[262]
1893	♦William K. Kellogg begins to manufacture health food products[263]
1894	♦Sadler becomes a salesman for Kellogg health food products[264]

---

[254] Harry P. Harrison, *Culture Under Canvas* (New York: Hastings House Pub., 1958), 82.

[255] Meussling, 68.

[256] Meussling, 64.

[257] *National Cyclopaedia of American Biography* (Clifton, N.J.: James T. White & Co., 1973) Vol. 54, 418 (see Appendix B of this book).

[258] *The Complete Edgar Cayce Readings*, Document #3780, 0254-001 Reports, (2/13/11).

[259] Charles Francis Horner, *The Life of James Redpath and the Development of the Modern Lyceum* (Newark, N. J.: Barse & Hopkins [c1926]) 284, 287.

[260] Meussling, 23.

[261] Meussling, 24.

[262] Horner, 284, 287.

[263] Meussling, 25.

[264] Meussling, 25.

Year	Event
1895	♦Sadler moves to Chicago as secretary for Chicago Medical Mission[265]
	♦Cayce meets Dwight Moody, gives up plan to become a minister[266]
1896	♦Sadler enrolled in Moody Bible Institute[267]
1897	♦Sadler marries Lena Kellogg, niece of John Harvey Kellogg[268]
	♦Cayce proposes to Gertrude Evans[269]
1899	♦Sadler becomes licensed minister of Seventh Day Adventists[270]
1901	♦Cayce gives first reading[271]
	♦Harry Loose becomes Illinois State Police officer[272]
	♦Newspaper article about Cayce[273]
	♦Cayce meets osteopath Al Layne[274]
	♦Sadler becomes an ordained minister[275]

[265] Meussling, 26.
[266] *The Complete Edgar Cayce Readings*, Document #3780, 0254-001 Reports, (2/13/11).
[267] Meussling, 27.
[268] Meussling, 27.
[269] *The Complete Edgar Cayce Readings*, Document #3780, 0254-001 Reports, (2/13/11).
[270] Meussling, 24.
[271] *The Complete Edgar Cayce Readings*, Document #3780, 0254-001 Reports, (2/13/11).
[272] Gardner, 138.
[273] Kentucky *New Era*, March, 1901. (see *Edgar Cayce's Photographic Legacy* by David M. Leary, 28).
[274] Sugrue, 105.
[275] Meussling, 24.

Year	Event
1902	◆Cayce moves to Bowling Green, KY[276]
	◆Cayce invents a stock market game called "Pit"[277]
1903	◆Cayce marries Gertrude Evans[278]
	◆EQB Literary Club is formed in Bowling Green, KY[279]
	◆"Cayce remembers nothing when he wakes up"[280]
1904	◆Traveling Chautauquas take to the road[281]
(year?)	◆John Harvey Kellogg is an early Chautauqua lecturer[282]
1905	◆Sadler gives his first Chautauqua speech[283]
	◆Chautauqua tent first erected in Hopkinsville, KY[284]
	◆Chicago AMA rules against doctors speaking publicly[285]
	◆Sadler believes in public communication[286]
1906	◆Mr. & Mrs. Sadler graduate medical school together[287]
	◆Sadler & wife begin giving lectures away from Chicago[288]

[276] *The Complete Edgar Cayce Readings*, Document #3780, 0254-001 Reports (2/13/11).
[277] Cayce, *Venture Inward*, 15.
[278] *The Complete Edgar Cayce Readings*, Document #3780, 0254-001 Reports (2/13/11).
[279] James Lewie Harman, *History of the E.Q.B. Club* (Bowling Green, Ky.: [s.n.], 1930.) 7.
[280] Cayce, *Venture Inward*, 15-16.
[281] Harrison, xvii.
[282] Meussling, 13.
[283] Meussling, ii, 21, 28, 102.
[284] Statement of D.D. Cayce and William Turner, Christian County Historian, Christian County, Ky.
[285] Meussling, 6.
[286] Meussling, 8.
[287] Meussling, 28.
[288] Meussling, 10.

Year	Event
	♦ Cayce gives demonstration before large audience -- out of town doctors present[289]
	♦ Contact person is a man approaching middle age[290]
	♦ Cayce is stuck with pins by unnamed doctor[291]
	♦ Dr.'s William & Lena Sadler observe contact person in trance[292]
	♦ Sadler sticks pins into unnamed contact person[293]
	♦ Harry Loose becomes a Chicago Police officer[294]
	♦ Urantia phenomenon begins this year, per Harold Sherman[295]
	♦ Urantia phenomenon begins this year, per Mark Kulieke[296]
	♦ Urantia phenomenon begins this year, per Harry Loose[297]
	♦ Urantia phenomenon begins this year, per Sadler's papers[298]

---

[289] Millard, 95.
    Sugrue, 137.
[290] Sherman, 62.
[291] Millard, 95.
    Sugrue, 137.
[292] Sherman, 62.
[293] Sherman, 62.
[294] Gardner, 138.
[295] Sherman, 62.
[296] Kulieke, 6, 18.
[297] Sherman, 38.
[298] Dr. Sadler's papers (see Appendix A of this book), "How the Urantia Papers Started," 198.

Year	Event
1906 (Con't)	◆Sleeping subject was married at this time[299]
	◆Cayce -- age 29 – approaching middle age based upon current mortality tables[300]
	◆Life expectancy for a white male is 48.2 yrs. (1900-1902 mortality tables)[301]
	◆Sadler announces he will give lectures and write books[302]
1907	◆Sadler & wife give Chautauqua lectures in Appleton, WI[303]
	◆Bill Sadler, Jr. born[304]
	◆Sadler founds Institute of Physiologic Therapeutics[305]
	◆"The Sadler lectures: Popular Health Lectures" -- Chautauqua publication[306]
	◆Hugh Lynn Cayce born[307]
(year?)	◆John Harvey Kellogg involved with Jane Addams at Hull House[308]
	◆Harry Loose involved with Hull House[309]
1908	◆Wilkins hired as cinematographer[310]

---

[299] Sherman, 62.
[300] *The Complete Edgar Cayce Readings*, 0254-001 Reports.
[301] Meussling, 3.
[302] Meussling, 167.
[303] Meussling, 10.
[304] Meussling, 28.
[305] Meussling, 36.
[306] *The Lyceumite & Talent*, V & VI (Sept. 1907), 2, inside cover.
[307] *The Complete Edgar Cayce Readings*, Document #3780, 0254-001 Reports (2/13/11).
[308] Meussling, 29.
[309] Gardner, 138.
[310] Wilkins Archives, Ohio State University.

Year	Event
	♦Sadler lectures in towns a safe distance from Chicago[311]
1909	♦Sadler forms the Chicago Institute of Research and Diagnosis[312]
	♦Sadler article in Chautauqua magazine[313]
	♦Cayce goes to Alabama[314]
1910	♦Cayce moves back to Hopkinsville[315]
	♦Article about Cayce appears in the New York *Times*[316]
	♦Hearst sends Roswell Field to Hopkinsville to interview Cayce[317]
	♦Wilkins learns to fly[318]
	♦Letter from Dr. Wesley H. Ketchum to American Association of Clinical Research about Cayce [319]

---

[311] Meussling, 10.

[312] Sadler, *Mind at Mischief*, vii.

[313] Meussling, 102, 104.

[314] *The Complete Edgar Cayce Readings*, Document #3780, 0254-001 Reports (2/13/11).

[315] *The Complete Edgar Cayce Readings*, Document #3780, 0254-001 Reports (2/13/11).

[316] Sugrue, 151.

[317] Sugrue, 163.

[318] Wilkins Archives, Ohio State University, box 18, folder 10 -- fact sheet on Wilkins (17 of 18 about the TV series by Sherman & Wilkins entitled "Explorers of the Mind").

[319] Sugrue, 151.

Year	Event
1910 (Con't)	◆*New York Times* & other newspapers across the country print Cayce's story[320]
	◆International Lyceum Association publishes article about Sadler[321]
	◆Sadler writes to Harry P. Harrison, manager of Redpath Chautauqua[322]
	◆Harry P. Harrison writes to Sadler[323]
1911	◆Cayce reading references beginning of "ethereal project"[324]
	◆Hearst invites Cayce to Chicago[325]
	◆Cayce visits Institute in Chicago[326]
	◆Sadler begins to study the sleeping subject[327]
	◆Cayce reading first recommends Kellogg's health food product[328]
	◆Sadler makes trip to England & Vienna to study psychiatry[329]
	◆Sadler begins to give public addresses on spiritualism[330]
	◆Sadler writes to Harry P. Harrison, Lyceum & Chautauqua[331]

---

[320] Sugrue, 151.

[321] Meussling, 59.

[322] Meussling, 74, 98.

[323] Meussling, 98.

[324] *The Complete Edgar Cayce Readings*, Document #3780, 0254-001 Text, (2/13/11).

[325] Sugrue, 164.

[326] *The Complete Edgar Cayce Readings*, Document # , 2155-004 Reports.

[327] Sadler, *Mind at Mischief*, appendix, 383.

[328] *The Complete Edgar Cayce Readings*, Document #, 3893-001 Text.

[329] Meussling, 11, 171.

[330] Meussling, 41.

[331] Meussling, 58.

Year	Event
1911 (Con't)	◆Sadler becomes Chairman of International Lyceum Association Program Committee[332]
	◆Sadler article appears in *Chautauqua Talent* magazine[333]
1912	◆Dr. Hugo Munsterberg investigates Cayce in Hopkinsville, KY[334]
	◆Wilfred Kellogg gets married[335]
	◆Sadler lectures Winona Lake, IN International Lyceum[336]
	◆Hopkinsville & Bowling Green, KY each have Chautauqua meetings[337]
	◆Cayce moves to Selma, AL[338]

[332] Meussling, 58.
[333] *The Lyceumite & Talent*, V, no. 3, Aug. 1911, "Personal: Dr. William S. Sadler: Surgeon, Author and Teacher", 7.
The Lyceumite & Talent, III, no. 8, Jan. 1910, "Give Your Audience Fresh Air", 9-10.
[334] Sugrue, 9-11.
[335] Gardner, 98.
[336] Meussling, 59.
[337] Harrison, 90.
[338] *The Complete Edgar Cayce Readings*, Document #, 0254-001 Reports.

Year	Event
1917	◆Sadler writes letter to Chautauqua recommending Harry Loose as a lecturer[339]
	◆Wilfred Kellogg is Sadler's business manager[340]
	◆Sadler & Kellogg correspond with Harry P. Harrison of Redpath Chautauqua[341]
1918	◆Sadler writes to Harry P. Harrison[342]
1921	◆Harry Loose lectures for Chautauqua in Marion, IN[343]
	◆Harold Sherman interviews Harry Loose for Marion *Chronicle* newspaper[344]
	◆Houdini lectures on spiritualistic fraud, University of Illinois[345]
1922	◆Harold Sherman loses contact with Harry Loose[346]
	◆Cayce advocates spirituality, not spiritualism[347]
1923	◆Cayce in Chicago[348]
	◆Dr. Sadler meets with Howard Thurston, famous magician[349]
	◆Sadler's Form begins in October[350]
	◆Cayce gives first metaphysical reading October[351]

[339] Gardner, 137.
[340] Meussling, 115.
[341] Meussling, 115.
[342] Meussling, 118, 119.
[343] Gardner, 135.
[344] Gardner, 135.
[345] Kellock, *Houdini: His Life Story*, 326.
[346] Sherman, 37.
[347] Birmingham *Age Herald* newspaper (see *Edgar Cayce's Photographic Legacy* by David M. Leary).
[348] *The Complete Edgar Cayce Readings*, Documents #45766, 45102, 45896, 1146, 38970, 45862, 45890.
[349] Sadler, *The Truth about Spiritualism*.
[350] Kulieke, 6.
[351] *The Complete Edgar Cayce Readings*, Document #, 5717-001 Background, (10/11/23).

Year	Event
	♦ Messages from sleeping subject are written and ver-bal[352]
	♦ Reading says Cayce writes while in sleep-like trance[353]
	♦ Reading says thought transference is being shown in evolution[354]
	♦ Cayce reading reveals sources[355]
	♦ Cayce readings are from Universal Forces[356]
1924	♦ Houdini states he has never found even one genuine case of psychic phenomena[357]
	♦ Houdini represents himself as an expert psychic investigator[358]
	♦ Cayce in Chicago[359]
	♦ Readings advise Cayce to go to Norfolk, VA[360]
	♦ AMA ruling threatening expulsion of doctors involved with Cayce's readings[361]

[352] Kulieke, 5.
Sadler, *Mind at Mischief*, 383.
[353] *The Complete Edgar Cayce Readings*, Document #, 3744-002.
[354] *The Complete Edgar Cayce Readings*, Document #, 3744-002.
[355] *The Complete Edgar Cayce Readings*, Document #, 3744-002.
[356] *The Complete Edgar Cayce Readings*, Document #, 3744-002.
[357] Harry Houdini, *Houdini: A Magician Among the Spirits* (New York: Arno, 1924).
[358] William L. Gresham, *Houdini: The Man Who Walked Through Walls* (New York: Holt, Rinehart, and Winston, 1929), 240.
[359] *The Complete Edgar Cayce Readings*, Documents #3808, 45650, 45654, 45658, 48799, 26363, 45662, 45990, 45178, 18722, 45666, 37562, 38974, 48830, 10374, 238, 38982, 39918, 49878, 56722, 56794, 48798, 48880, 50438, 50602, 50604, 486, 45670, 50198, 23758, 3814, 6474, 51708.
[360] *The Complete Edgar Cayce Readings*, Document #0254-008.
[361] *The Complete Edgar Cayce Readings*, Document #51704, 4905-002 Reports, Letter to Cayce from Mr. Gumbinsky dated 8/26/24.

Year	Event
(year?)	♦ Sadler calls in Houdini & Thurston to help investigate sleeping subject[362]
	♦ Houdini & Thurston unable to give explanation of phenomenon of sleeping subject[363]
	♦ Cayce gives demonstration for Houdini[364]
	♦ Houdini unable to give explanation of phenomenon of Cayce[365]
1925	♦ Urantia Forum begins to operate under secrecy[366]
	♦ Houdini performs in Chicago for eight weeks[367]
	♦ Cayce in Chicago[368]
	♦ Houdini and his staff investigate 40 mediums while in Chicago[369]
	♦ Cayce moves to Virginia Beach[370]
1926	♦ Houdini's death
	♦ Sadler ends his career as a Chautauqua lecturer[371]
	♦ Death of Cayce's mother[372]

[362] Sherman, 64.

[363] Sherman, 64.

[364] *The Complete Edgar Cayce Readings*, Document #13576, 0464-013 Reports, Cayce letter to Mrs. [464] dated 2/21/33.

[365] *The Complete Edgar Cayce Readings*, Document #13576, 0464-013 Reports, Cayce letter to Mrs. [464] dated 2/21/33.

[366] Kulieke, 8.
      Dr. Sadler's papers (see Appendix A of this book), "The Forum Becomes a Closed Group," 200.

[367] Christopher, *Houdini: A Pictorial Life*, 166-72.

[368] *The Complete Edgar Cayce Readings*, Document #51752, 4905-014 Reports, (2/23/25 letter).

[369] Christopher, *Houdini: A Pictorial Life*.

[370] *The Complete Edgar Cayce Readings*, Document #3780, 0254-001 Reports, (2/13/11).

[371] Meussling, ii, 2.

[372] *The Complete Edgar Cayce Readings*, Document #3780, 0254-001 Reports, (2/13/11).

Year	Event
(year?)	♦ Sadler consults Wilkins[373]
1927	♦ Wilkins meets with Hearst[374]
	♦ Cayce in Chicago[375]
	♦ Sadler's sleeping subject advises listeners to ask more meaningful questions (This happened *about* 20 years after the contact process began in 1906)[376]
	♦ The sleeping Cayce advises his listeners to ask more meaningful questions[377]
1928	♦ Wilkins names his Antarctic discoveries Hearst Land and Casey Channel[378]
	♦ Cayce in Chicago[379]
(year?)	♦ Wilkins in Norfolk, VA[380]
1929	♦ *The Mind at Mischief* published by Hearst's publishing company, Funk & Wagnalls[381]
	♦ Sadler has attended approximately 250 sessions with the sleeping subject[382]

---

[373] Kulieke, 4.

[374] Thomas, 122.

[375] *The Complete Edgar Cayce Readings*, Documents #55988, 22226, 51976, 2658.

[376] Dr. Sadler's papers (see Appendix A of this book) "How the Urantia Papers Started", 198.

[377] *The Complete Edgar Cayce Readings*, Document #57054, 5756-004, #12, (3/17/27).

[378] Thomas, 127.

[379] *The Complete Edgar Cayce Readings*, Documents #47304, 56775, 35794, 49806, 50350, 50354, 56442, 56434, 22318, 1538, 51102, 2682, 33420, 46696, 30832, 27520.

[380] Wilkins Archives, Ohio State University, box 2, folder 3 -- letters Wilkins wrote from the Monticello Hotel.

[381] Sadler, *Mind at Mischief*, title page.

[382] Sadler, *Mind at Mischief*, 383.

Year	Event
1929 (con't)	♦ *The Mind at Mischief* states that the sleeping subject remembers nothing when he wakes up[383]
	♦ Reading refers to three deceased human authors who wish to speak[384]
1930	♦ Sadler begins specializing in psychiatry[385]
	♦ Cayce in Chicago[386]
	♦ Wilkins in Chicago[387]
	♦ Sadler begins teaching at McCormick Theological Seminary[388]
1931	♦ Cayce in Chicago[389]
	♦ Association for Research and Enlightenment is formed[390]
1932	♦ Cayce in Chicago (Spring time)[391]
	♦ Wilkins in Chicago (Spring time)[392]

---

[383] Sadler, *Mind at Mischief*, 383.

[384] *The Complete Edgar Cayce Readings*, Document #57066, 5756-007 Text, (4/10/29).

[385] *National Cyclopaedia of American Biography*, Vol. 54, 418 (see Appendix B of this book).

[386] *The Complete Edgar Cayce Readings*, Document #2686, 0165-005 Text, (8/27/28).

[387] Wilkins Archives, Ohio State University, box 12, folder 20 -- letter to Wilkins from John Borden dated 11/15/30.

[388] Meussling, 45.

[389] *The Complete Edgar Cayce Readings*, Document #35116, #2123-001 Reports, (8/31/31).

[390] *The Complete Edgar Cayce Readings*, Document #3780, 0254-001 Reports, (2/13/11).

[391] *The Complete Edgar Cayce Readings*, Documents #35116, 35348, 35356.

[392] Wilkins Archives, Ohio State University, box 12, folder 22 -- letter to Wilkins from the Emerson Bureau dated 3/22/32 regarding speaking engagements for Wilkins scheduled for April in Chicago.

Year	Event
	◆Cayce reading names its source as the Universal Consciousness[393]
	◆Cayce reading says Jesus was a musician and played the harp[394]
	◆End of Chautauquas[395]
1933	◆Cayce admits giving demonstration for Houdini[396]
	◆Cayce in Chicago[397]
	◆Cayce reading says that the Prince of Peace (Jesus) was a harpist[398]
	◆Cayce recommends books and authors while in trance[399]
1934	◆Reading describes source of Cayce's information[400]
	◆Parts I & II of the Urantia manuscript completed[401]
	◆Cayce in Chicago[402]
	◆Prayer written by Wilkins for himself included in *The Urantia Book*, paper 48[403]

[393] *The Complete Edgar Cayce Readings*, Document #8360, 0294-131 Reports, "How Edgar Cayce gives a Psychic Reading" by Hugh Lynn Cayce (1/33).
[394] *The Complete Edgar Cayce Readings*, Document #56914, 5749-001 Text, #13, (6/14/32).
[395] Meussling, 169.
[396] *The Complete Edgar Cayce Readings*, Document #13576, 0464-013 Reports, EC's letter dated 2/21/33.
[397] *The Complete Edgar Cayce Readings*, Documents #10772, 47872, 35976.
[398] *The Complete Edgar Cayce Readings*, Document #6953, 0275-035 Text, #10, (11/21/33).
[399] *The Complete Edgar Cayce Readings*, Document #13062, 0440-007, #13 & 14 (12/21/33).
[400] *The Complete Edgar Cayce Readings*, Documents #57042, 8360, 57094 (#5) 45026 (#11).
[401] *The Urantia Book*, 648.
[402] *The Complete Edgar Cayce Readings*, Documents #16360, 37440, 18248.
[403] Thomas, 295.

Year	Event
1934 (con't)	◆Eileen Garrett (famous psychic) receives reading from Cayce[404]
	◆Cayce recommends books & authors while in trance[405]
1935	◆Cayce warns against world war[406]
	◆Part III of the Urantia manuscript completed[407]
	◆Edgar Evans Cayce goes to Duke University[408]
1936	◆Thurston's death
	◆Part 4 of the Urantia manuscript is completed[409]
	◆Urantia manuscript states that Jesus played the harp[410]
	◆Cayce in Chicago[411]
	◆Hearst writes letter to Wilkins[412]
	◆Cayce meets with parapsychologists Dr.'s Rhine & Murphy[413]

[404] *The Complete Edgar Cayce Readings*, Document #14526, 0507-001 Text (2/3/34).

[405] *The Complete Edgar Cayce Readings*, Document #13078, 0440-011 Text, #28 (1/9/34).

[406] Cayce, *Venture Inward*, 69.

[407] *The Urantia Book*, 1319.

[408] *The Complete Edgar Cayce Readings*, Document #3780, 0254-001 Reports, (12/13/11).

[409] Dr. Sadler's papers (see Appendix A of this book) "Receiving the Completed Papers", 202.

[410] Urantia Book, 1364, 1387, 1389, 1402.

[411] *The Complete Edgar Cayce Readings*, Document #33167, 1870-001 Background, 6/22/37 letter to EC.

[412] Wilkins Archives, Ohio State University, box 12, folder 26, letter dated 5/22/36.

[413] *The Complete Edgar Cayce Readings*, Document #3780, 0254-001 Reports, and Document #32560, 1800-026 Reports, 18.

Year	Event
1936 (con't)	◆ Dr. Warner of Duke University becomes member of ARE[414]
	◆ Dr. Rhine of Duke University gets reading for his daughter[415]
1937	◆ Harold Sherman and Sir Hubert Wilkins conduct long distance ESP experiments[416]
	◆ Death of Cayce's father[417]
1938	◆ Harold Sherman & Hugh Lynn Cayce begin radio program[418]
	◆ Harold Sherman requests health reading from Cayce[419]
1939	◆ Harold Sherman & Sir Hubert Wilkins write article for *Cosmopolitan* magazine[420]
	◆ The Seventy -- Urantia study group begins[421]
	◆ Harold Sherman requests two additional health readings from Cayce[422]
	◆ Harold Sherman requests a life reading from Cayce[423]

[414] *The Complete Edgar Cayce Readings*, Document #32556, 1800-025 Reports, 29.

[415] *The Complete Edgar Cayce Readings*, Document #32556, 1800-025 Reports, 29.

[416] Wilkins, *Thoughts Through Space*. This entire book documents the experiments carried out by Sherman and Wilkins.

[417] *The Complete Edgar Cayce Readings*, Document #3780, 0254-001 Reports (12/13/11).

[418] *The Complete Edgar Cayce Readings*, Document #4182, 0254-0102 Text (10/6/38).

[419] *The Complete Edgar Cayce Readings*, Document #31670, 1724-001 Text (11/2/38) -- Sherman's identification number was 1724.

[420] Sherman, 37.

[421] Dr. Sadler's papers (see Appendix A of this book) "The Seventy", 208.

[422] *The Complete Edgar Cayce Readings*, Document #31674, 1724-002, and Document #32678, 1704-003.

[423] *The Complete Edgar Cayce Readings*, Document #31682, 1724-004.

212   APPENDIX D

Year	Event
1939 (con't)	♦ Harold Sherman & Edgar Cayce write letters to each other[424]
	♦ Wilkins receives telephone call from William W. Kellogg[425]
	♦ Cayce in Chicago[426]
1940	♦ Cayce predicts America will be involved in World War II, six months in advance[427]
	♦ Wilkins in Chicago (October)[428]
	♦ Sherman writes letter to Wilkins[429]
	♦ Wilkins in Chicago (November)[430]
1941	♦ Loose living in Montgomery Park, CA[431]
	♦ Loose writes letter to Sherman predicting US involvement in war 3 months in advance of Pearl Harbor attack[432]
	♦ Sherman & Hugh Lynn Cayce correspond by mail[433]
	♦ Sherman goes to Hollywood, CA and visits Loose in Montgomery Park[434]
	♦ Loose tells Sherman of Urantia project in Chicago[435]
	♦ Sherman goes to Chicago and meets Sadler and joins Forum[436]

[424] *The Complete Edgar Cayce Readings*, 1724 Reports (series).
[425] Wilkins Archives, Ohio State University, box 12, folder 29.
[426] *The Complete Edgar Cayce Readings*, Document #32624, 1807-001 Reports (1/31/39).
[427] Cayce, *Venture Inward*, 71.
[428] Wilkins Archives, Ohio State University, box 12, folder 31.
[429] Wilkins Archives, Ohio State University, box 12, folder 31.
[430] Wilkins Archives, Ohio State University, box 12, folder 34.
[431] Sherman, 37.
[432] Sherman, 38.
[433] *The Complete Edgar Cayce Readings*, 1724 Reports (series).
[434] Sherman, 41.
[435] Sherman, 38, 57.
[436] Sherman, 59.

Year	Event
1941 (con't)	♦ Sherman goes back to California & tells Loose that he joined Sadler's Forum[437]
	♦ Pearl Harbor is attacked
	♦ America is involved in WWII
	♦ Harry Loose letter to Sherman (2/4/41) states Urantia phenomenon began 35 years ago.[438]
1942	♦ Sherman leaves California and moves to Chicago to study Urantia Papers[439]
	♦ Sadler tells Mr. & Mrs. Sherman beginning date of Urantia phenomenon was "*about* 35 years ago", and reveals details about the sleeping subject[440]
	♦ Sadler admits consulting Houdini[441]
	♦ Loose and Sherman correspond by mail about the Urantia manuscript[442]

[437] Sherman, 60.
[438] Sherman, 38.
[439] Sherman, 59.
[440] Sherman, 62-65.
[441] Sherman, 64.
[442] Gardner, 151.

Year	Event
1943	♦Loose continues to write to Sherman in Chicago through 1943[443]
	♦Loose dies[444]
	♦Forum member (Mrs. 3316) receives health reading from Edgar Cayce[445]
	♦ *There is a River: The Story of Edgar Cayce* is published[446]
1944	♦Member of Sadler's Forum (Mrs. 3316) writes to Cayce[447]
1945	♦Cayce's death[448]
	♦Sir Hubert Wilkins is a Chautauqua lecturer, receives letter from Harry P. Harrison[449]
1946	♦Letter written to Wilkins from one of his friends with comments referencing Chicago manuscript[450]
1947	♦Sherman leaves Chicago[451]
1948	♦Dr. J.B. Rhine of Duke University becomes interested in Wilkins[452]

---

[443] Sherman, 38.

[444] Sherman, 57.

[445] *The Complete Edgar Cayce Readings*, Document #42980, 3316-001 Text (10/27/43).

[446] *The Complete Edgar Cayce Readings*, Document #3780, 0254-001 Reports (2/13/11).

[447] *The Complete Edgar Cayce Readings*, Document #42980, 3316-001 Reports (10/27/43).

[448] *The Complete Edgar Cayce Readings*, Document #3780, 0254-001 Reports (2/13/11).

[449] Wilkins Archives, Ohio State University, box 12, folder 36 -- letter dated 10/9/45.

[450] Wilkins Archives, Ohio State University, box 12, folder 37 -- letter dated 3/14/46.

[451] Sherman, 86.

[452] Wilkins Archives, Ohio State University, box 12, folder 39 -- letter from Sherman to Wilkins dated 9/3/48.

Year	Event
	♦ Eileen Garret (famous psychic) lectures in New York City at ARE group[453]
	♦ Eileen Garret has worked for Dr. Rhine for 13 years[454]
	♦ Sherman writes letter to Eileen Garret[455]
1949	♦ Sherman and Hugh Lynn Cayce correspond by mail[456]
	♦ Wilkins reports on points from the Chicago Forum to a friend[457]
1950	♦ Member of Sadler's Forum (Mrs. 3316) attends ARE conference at Virginia Beach[458]
	♦ Wilkins contributes $1,000 for publication of *Urantia Book*[459]
	♦ Sadler writes letter to Wilkins about *Urantia Book* publication[460]
	♦ (very next day) Sherman writes letter to Wilkins about *Urantia Book* publication[461]

---

[453] *The Complete Edgar Cayce Readings*, Document #14532, 0507-002 Reports (2/6/34).

[454] *The Complete Edgar Cayce Readings*, Document #14532, 0507-002 Reports (2/6/34).

[455] Wilkins Archives, Ohio State University, box 12, folder 39 -- referenced in letter from Sherman to Wilkins dated 8/13/48.

[456] *The Complete Edgar Cayce Readings*, 1724 Reports (series).

[457] Wilkins Archives, Ohio State University, box 12, folder 41 -- letter dated 1/9/49.

[458] *The Complete Edgar Cayce Readings*, Document #42980, 3316-001 Reports (10/27/43).

[459] Wilkins Archives, box 12, folder 42 -- letter from Sadler to Wilkins dated 12/15/1950.

[460] Wilkins Archives, box 12, folder 42 -- letter from Sadler to Wilkins dated 12/15/1950.

[461] Wilkins Archives, box 12, folder 42 -- letter from Sherman to Wilkins dated 12/16/1950.

Year	Event
1950 (con't)	◆Sherman claims to Wilkins that parts of *The Book of Urantia* were tampered with[462]
	◆Bill Sadler, Jr. writes to Wilkins[463]
1951	◆Hearst's death[464]
	◆Wilkins receives letter from a friend asking him, "Are Urantia Papers are still a secret to the chosen few 20-30 people?"[465]
1952	◆Sherman & Hugh Lynn Cayce correspond by mail[466]
1953	◆Member of Sadler's Forum (Mrs. 3316) writes letter to ARE[467]
1955	◆*Urantia Book* published[468]
	◆Wilkins associated with *Urantia Book* for many years[469]
	◆Member of Urantia Brotherhood (Mrs. 3316) mails *Urantia Book* to ARE[470]
	◆Sleeping subject never remembers anything if not told afterward, per Sadler[471]

[462] Wilkins Archives, box 12, folder 42 -- letter from Sherman to Wilkins dated 12/16/1950.

[463] Wilkins Archives, box 12, folder 42 -- letter dated 12/19/1950.

[464] Swanberg, W. A., *Citizen Hearst* (New York: Bantam Books, 1971) 617.

[465] Wilkins Archives, Box 12, folder 43 -- letter dated 9/13/1951.

[466] *The Complete Edgar Cayce Readings*, 1724 Reports (series).

[467] *The Complete Edgar Cayce Readings*, Document #42980, 3316-001 Reports (10/27/43).

[468] *The Urantia Book*, copyright information.

[469] Wilkins Archives, Ohio State University, box 13, folder 3 -- letter to Winston Ross dated 11/1/1955.

[470] *The Complete Edgar Cayce Readings*, Document #42980, 3316-001 Reports (10/27/43).

[471] Sadler, *Mind at Mischief*, appendix, 383.

Year	Event
1955 (con't)	◆Sleeping subject had no idea that he was used as medium for Urantia Papers, per Wilkins[472]
	◆Sherman in close contact with Dr. J.B. Rhine of Duke University[473]
	◆Difficulty with limitation of human language, per sleeping subject[474]
	◆Difficulty with limitation of human language, per sleeping Cayce[475]
1956	◆Wilfred Kellogg's death[476]
	◆Wilkins in Chicago[477]
	◆Wilkins references 'thought adjuster' in letter to Dr. Goresline[478]
1957	◆Sherman writes letter to Wilkins stating that he knows that some of the information in *The Urantia Book* is not from the original source[479]
1958	◆Wilkins death[480]
1960	◆The book *Sir Hubert Wilkins: Enigma of Exploration* is published[481]

---

[472] Wilkins Archives, Ohio State University, box 13, folder 3 -- letter to Winston Ross dated 11/1/1955.
    Grierson, 202.
[473] Wilkins Archives, Ohio State University, box 18, folder 10 -- letter from Duna Gregory to Edward R. Murrow dated 3/20/55.
[474] *The Urantia Book*, foreword, para. 2.
[475] *The Complete Edgar Cayce Readings*, Document #4028, 0254-063 Reports (4/26/32).
[476] Gardner, 101.
[477] Wilkins Archive, Ohio State University, box 13, folder 4.
[478] Wilkins Archive, Ohio State University, box 13, folder 4.
[479] Wilkins Archive, Ohio State University, box 13, folder 5 -- letter from Sherman to Wilkins dated 2/10/57.
[480] Grierson, 210.
[481] Grierson, 3.

Year	Event
1960 (con't)	◆ Wilkins is named as one of the contributors to *The Urantia Book*[482]
1962	◆ Bill Sadler, Jr. reveals details about the origin of *The Urantia Book*[483]
	◆ Sleeping subject was a businessman[484]
	◆ Sleeping subject not interested in predicting stocks[485]
	◆ Sleeping subject not interested in locating lost objects[486]
	◆ Sleeping subject not interested in predicting the winners of horse races[487]
	◆ Bill Sadler, Jr. states the handwriting of sleeping subject, while asleep, is clearly identifiable as his own[488]
	◆ Dr. William Sadler states that handwriting experts determined handwriting of sleeping subject, while asleep, was definitely *not* identifiable as his own[489]
1969	◆ Sadler dies[490]
1974	◆ *How to Know What to Believe* by Harold Sherman is published
1977	◆ Sherman letter claims Sadler changed *Urantia Book* text[491]

[482] Grierson, 8.
[483] Elliott, Berkley, tape recording made of interview with Bill Sadler, Jr., unpublished.
[484] Elliott tape.
[485] Elliott tape.
[486] Elliott tape.
[487] Elliott tape.
[488] Elliott tape.
[489] Kulieke, 6.
[490] Meussling, 60.
[491] Letter to David Kruse, from Harold Sherman, unpublished.

Year	Event
1983	♦ *Analysis of a Revealed Text: The Urantia Book* is written, referencing Cayce[492]
1987	♦ Harold Sherman's death
1991	♦ *Birth of a Revelation* by Mark Kulieke is published
1992	♦ Bud Kagan states in a deposition that Bill Sadler, Jr. told him the sleeping subject was not a Kellogg[493]
1994	♦ Bill Sadler, Jr. named as contributor to *Urantia Book*[494]
1995	♦ *Urantia: The Great Cult Mystery* by Martin Gardner is published
1996	♦ Matthew Block identifies over 100 different source books used in *The Urantia Book*[495]
1998	♦ Bud Bromley conducts coefficient of correlation test using geographical list of ancient Sumerian cities compared to references of same from *Urantia Book* & Cayce readings and finds 0.99666 percent probability that some one factor caused the similarity of both lists. No possibility of random chance.

---

[492] Rheaume, Jacques, "Analysis of a Revealed Text: *The Urantia Book*", 32. [Written in French for the University of Ottawa, Canada, 1983: "The information coming through the subject was both written and oral but that's all the information Dr. Sadler gave about it. The man talked during his sleep-and remembered nothing of what happened when he awoke. One can think of Edgar Cayce, who matches the description. But as the contact group always worked in Chicago and since Cayce traveled so much over the years, we can rule him out despite certain resemblances."]

[493] Gardner, 130.

[494] See copyright renewal forms submitted to U.S. Office of Copyrights by Urantia Foundation.

[495] *Spiritual Fellowship Journal*, Fall, 1993.
   Gardner, Chap. 16.
   Continuing research by Matthew Block, unpublished at the time of this printing.

Appendix E: Ancient Mesopotamian Cities

On the following page is a list of known ancient Mesopotamian cities, which was compiled from a map of that geographic region. The numbers in the columns show how many times the city is mentioned in the Cayce readings and *The Urantia Book*. (See p. 32 for information about the Coefficient of Correlation test done on these numbers.)

CITY	CAYCE	URANTIA BOOK
Hatusha	0	0
Hatti	0	0
Carcheemish	0	0
Urarit	0	0
Byblos	0	0
Canaan	1	3
Jerusalem	194	495
Jericho	15	44
Martu	0	0
Urartu	0	0
Dur Sharru Kin	0	0
Harran	0	0
Mitanni	0	0
Mari	0	0
Neneveh	0	0
Nineveh	1	1
Nimrud	0	0
Ashur	1	1
Assyria	2	7
Nuzi	0	0
Eshnuna	0	0
Babylon	6	19
Akkad	0	2
Susa	1	4
Elam	2	2
Sumer	0	1
Sippar	0	0
Kish	4	6
Nippur	0	0
Adab	0	0
Umma	0	0
Shutuppak	0	0
Lagash	0	1
Ur	22	17
El-Ubaid	0	0
Eridu	0	0

Appendix F: Words and Ideas from *The Principles of Nature, Her Divine Revelations, and a Voice to Mankind*

p.   91   idea of reincarnation or resurrection
p.   96   concentric circles
p. 108   concentric circles
p. 109   the idea that all matter force and energy are one
p. 112   concentric circles
p. 118   the doctrine of concentric circles
p. 123   corporeal
p. 126   concentric circles
p. 130   the stationary center of infinite space
p. 131   concentric circles
p. 133   concentric circles
p. 137   concentric circles
p. 139   the idea that all matter, force, and energy is one
p. 142   concentric circles
p. 146   a symbol is described that illustrates the Beginning: a circle with a dot in the center. This is also an Egyptian symbol derived from other more ancient sources.
p. 153   concentric circles
p. 160   here the book describes the size, location, revolution, velocity, etc., of the planet known as Pluto. Pluto was not discovered until 1933.
p. 161   the sleeping subject gives information from an as yet unpublished book manuscript that was being written in another country across the ocean. The manuscript was later published and distributed in America and the information then was confirmed.
p. 166   corporeal
p. 185   conjoined
p. 188   homogenous
p. 191 vicissitudes
p. 336   contradistinction
p. 344   geological differences during the Earth's evolution
p. 345   references to previous inundations and catastrophes
p. 347   land submerged which was located in the middle of the Pacific Ocean
p. 348   reference to the biblical flood
p. 368   Latin language mentioned
p. 372   various languages mentioned including Latin
p. 374   use of Latin word 'minutae (various mention of 'ia' words throughout the text)

p. 377   Latin mentioned
p. 378   Zend Vest of Zoraster
p. 388   Sanskrit language mentioned
p. 389   Sanskrit language mentioned
p. 390   Latin mentioned
p. 391   biblical flood was not a universal deluge
p. 393   it was a subjective opinion that the flood was universal
p. 393   reference to valley that was submerged and is now the bed of
the
          Pacific Ocean
p. 394   the destruction sounds like Churchward's story of Mu
p. 395   Fohi was the Chinese version of Noah
p. 396   they believed they were the only tribe that was saved, supposing
          hat all other portions had sunk beneath the great waters
p. 399   The Jewish story of Noah also had a Chinese and Greek version.
          Fohi was Chinese, Xisuthrus was Chaldeanic-Persians,
          Delucalion was Greek, Scottavarata was Indian, and Noah was
          Jewish.
p. 403   Swedenborg mentioned in footnote
p. 412   The story of Adam and Eve and the Garden of Eden
p. 413   what is called natural death is not death but a mere change of
          organization
p. 455   Davis suggests book title while asleep -- sounds like Cayce
p. 493   No divine conception
p. 521   martyrdom of Jesus-sounds like UB
p. 522   reincarnation or anastasis means progressive reform. What
          words mean now are not what they meant originally.
p. 522   corporeal

224

Appendix G: The Sealed Urantia Archives

In early January 2000, Karen and I journeyed to The University of Central Arkansas to examine material that had been sealed many years earlier by Harold Sherman; the Urantia files. We met one other individual there for the unsealing of the Urantia material, his name was Ken Revel.

The archivist there had received word that someone might attempt to destroy the Urantia material, therefore there were certain restrictions placed upon all of us. We were only allowed to look at one folder at a time, we were watched by a staff member, at all times, and none of the material could be removed from the immediate area of the archives where we were examining it.

We discovered that Sherman had a close friendship with Hugh Lynn Cayce, Edgar Cayce's eldest son. Several months after completing the experiment in telepathy with Sir Hubert Wilkins (See Thoughts Through Space), Sherman became involved with Hugh Lynn Cayce in developing a radio program about the psychic readings given by Edgar Cayce. It was called Mysteries of the Mind.

We were surprised to discover a series of diaries that Sherman and his wife had kept during their association with Sadler's Forum. We copied the diaries and have forwarded them to Matthew Block. Matt plans to publish the contents of all of those diaries.

We were surprised to discover that all of the letters from Harry Loose to the Shermans had been removed from the archives. When we asked the archivist about this, he contacted Marcia Sherman, their daughter. She explained that she had removed the Loose letters. As time went by, I spoke with Marcia several times on the telephone. She said her sister had possession of the letters and would not allow anyone to see them.

From other material in the archives, we learned that Sherman had received personal readings from Cayce for his health. He also had one "life" reading. Some time earlier, I had read Sherman's book "How to Know What to Believe". In that book Sherman sharply criticized Cayce, but as I read the archived material, I discovered Sherman was very fond of Cayce. In his book, Sherman condemned Cayce for a reading he gave for Sherman. But in the archives, I discovered that Sherman revealed that Cayce's readings were correct. The problem was that at the time of Sherman's treatment, the physician's assistant who applied the use of an electrical appliance to him, mis-adjusted the settings and left the examination room during the treatment process. Sherman did not blame Cayce for this, if fact even after this event, Sherman still firmly believed in Cayce and wanted to get his own personal physician involved with Cayce to help prove that Cayce's psychic ability was genuine.

I also discovered a folder that contained information on three different topics of interest: The Urantia Book, Nature's Divine Revelations A Voice to Mankind, and Edgar Cayce. It seemed that Sherman was comparing each with the other looking for parallels they had in common with each other.

Within one folder, there was an outline for a book about Cayce that Sherman had been working on: There Is A River.

Initially, Cayce's biography was being written by Thomas Sugrue. Tom became ill and it was not known if Tom would recover, so Sherman began to work on Cayce's biography. However, Tom recovered and finished writing Cayce's life story. I believe that Sherman became bitter about this.

JB

Appendix H: Finding Dr. Vonne Meussling

John with Dr. Meussling

In the beginning of our search for information about the events leading up to the publication of the Urantia Book, which began in 1994, Karen and I traveled to Virginia Beach, Bowling Green University, Hopkinsville Kentucky, and Chicago, among other places. We were trying to piece together bits of information to develop an accurate account of past incidents linking Edgar Cayce with The Urantia Book. The trail was still fresh and some of the people whom we were able to contact were still living, like Edgar Evans Cayce, Delbert D. Cayce III, Meredith and Irene Sprunger, and Dr. Vonne Meussling.

Dr. Meredith Sprunger, PhD had talked to us much about Dr. William Sadler, MD of Chicago, Illinois, who had been so involved with the development of the Urantia Book. We learned that Dr. Sadler had been the first doctor to speak publicly about health issues, during a time in history when such things were not permitted by the American Medical Association, before the days of radio and television. Most Americans learned about current events by reading newspapers.

During this epoch in American history the word Chautauqua became a household word that was to change the country and then was to disappear as quickly as it came, about the time of the advent of automobiles and radio.

We discovered a doctoral thesis titled "William Sadler Chautauqua's Medic Orator," dated 1970, written by G. Vonne Meussling. We read her thesis and found it to be a gold mine of information. We thought that perhaps she might still have some records that she may have collected during the preparation of her thesis. We managed to contact her by telephone. To our disappointment, she told us that she had moved a couple of times since then and all of the records had been ruined by a flood in her basement. So that trail ended. By 1998, we published the first copy of *Edgar Cayce and the Urantia Book*.

By the year 2016, we began to read the thesis again and decided that it would be good if it was available for people who were interested in the history of Dr. Sadler's life. We sought to contact Dr. Vonne Meussling again, who would now be 90 years old. Bowling Green State University was the first place we contacted. The alumni department was unable to help us. So we contacted other schools where she had been a teacher, but were unable to acquire her current whereabouts or even her photo. We were afraid that perhaps she was no longer living.

Then Karen managed to locate her son Mark and we contacted him. He told us she was alive and well and living in a nearby community! Mark helped us contact her and we set an appointment to meet with her. Dr. Meussling is a wonderful person, very kind and helpful to us in our effort to publish her thesis. We are happy to have the opportunity to introduce her to you!

John Bunker
Churubusco, IN 3/30/2017

Bibliography

AGEE, DORIS. *Edgar Cayce on ESP*. New York: Warner Books, 1983.

ANDREWS, SHIRLEY. *Atlantis: Insights from a Lost Civilization*. St. Paul, Minn.: Llewellyn Publications, 1997.

BODE, CAROL. *The American Lyceum-Town Meeting of the Mind*. New York Oxford University Press, 1956.

BRO, HARMON H. *Begin a New Life*. New York: Harper & Row, 1971.

BRO, HARMON H. *Edgar Cayce on Religion and Psychic Experience*. New York: Paperback Library, 1970.

CAYCE, EDGAR EVANS. *Humor From the Psychic*. Virginia Beach, Va.: A.R.E. Press, 1990.

CAYCE, HUGH LYNN. *Venture Inward*. New York: Harper & Row, 1964.

CERMINARA, GINA. *Many Mansions*. New York: Morrow, 1967.

CHRISTOPHER, MATT. *Houdini: A Pictorial Life*. New York: Crowell, 1976.

CHRISTOPHER, MILBOURNE. *Houdini: Untold Story*. New York: Crowell, 1969.

CHRISTOPHER, MILBOURNE. *Houdini: His Life Story*. New York : Crowell, c1976.

The Complete Edgar Cayce Readings [CD-ROM]. Virginia Beach, Va.: A.R.E Press, 1993.

DAVIS, ANDREW JACKSON. The Principles of Nature, Her Divine Revelations, and A Voice to Mankind. Boston: Colby and Rich, 1886.

Encyclopaedia of the Celts, compiled & edited by Knud Mariboe, 1994.

FURST, JEFFREY. *Edgar Cayce's Story of Jesus*. New York: Coward-McCann, 1969.

GARDNER, MARTIN. *Urantia: The Great Cult Mystery*. Amherst, NY: Prometheus, 1995.

GIBSON, WALTER B. *The Original Houdini Scrapbook*. New York: Sterling, 1976.

GRESHAM, WILLIAM L. *Houdini: The Man Who Walked Through Walls*. New York: Holt, Rinehart and Winston, 1959.

GRIERSON, JOHN. *Sir Hubert Wilkins: Enigma of Exploration*. London: Robert Hale, [1959?].

HARMAN, JAMES LEWIE. *History of the E.Q.B. Club*. Bowling Green, Ky.: [s.n.], 1930.

HARRISON, HARRY P. *Culture Under Canvas*. New York: Hastings House Pub., 1958.

Holy Bible [King James Version]. Nashville: Thomas Nelson, Inc., 1978.

HORNER, CHARLES FRANCIS. *The Life of James Redpath and the Development of the Modern Lyceum*. Newark, N. J.: Barse & Hopkins [c1926].

HOUDINI, HARRY. *Houdini: A Magician Among the Spirits*. New York: Arno, 1972.

KELLOCK, HAROLD. *Houdini: His Life Story*. New York: Blue Ribbon Books, 1928.

KULIEKE, MARK. *Birth of a Revelation: The Story of the Urantia Papers*. Green Bay, Wisc.: Morning Star Foundation, 1994.

LEARY, DAVID M. *Edgar Cayce's Photographic Legacy*. New York: Doubleday, 1978.

MEUSSLING, G. VONNE. "William S. Sadler: Chautauqua's Medic Orator," diss., Bowling Green State University, 1970.

MILLARD, JOSEPH. *Edgar Cayce: Mystery Man of Miracles*. Greenwich, Conn.: Fawcett, 1967.

National Cyclopaedia of American Biography. Vol. 54. Clifton, N.J.: James T. White & Co., 1973.

Oxford Latin Dictionary. Oxford University Press, 1983.

PALMER, L.R. *The Latin Language*. London: Faber & Faber, Ltd., 1954.

READ, ANNE. *Edgar Cayce on Jesus and His Church*. New York: Paperback Library, 1970.

RHEAUME, JACQUES. "Analysis of a Revealed Text: *The Urantia Book*," diss. (orig. in French "Analyse D'un Texte Revele"), University of Ottawa, 1983.

ROBINSON, LYTLE. *Edgar Cayce's Story of the Origin and Destiny of Man*. New York: Coward, McCann & Geoghegan, Inc., 1972.

ROBINSON, LYTLE W. *Is it True What They Say About Edgar Cayce?* New York: Berkley Books, 1979.

SADLER, BILL, JR. Taped interview, 1962.

SADLER, WILLIAM S. *The Mind at Mischief*. New York: Funk & Wagnalls, 1929.

SADLER, WILLIAM S. *The Truth About Spiritualism*. Chicago: McClurg, 1923.

SADLER, WILLIAM S. *What every Salesman Should Know About His Health*. Chicago: American Publishers Corp., 1925.

SHERMAN, HAROLD. *How to Know What to Believe*. Greenwich: Fawcett, 1976.

SITCHIN, ZECHARIA. *The Stairway to Heaven*. New York: Avon, 1980.

The Spiritual Fellowship Journal. Fort Wayne, IN: The Christian Fellowship of Students of *The Urantia Book*.

STEARN, JESS. *A Prophet in His Own Country: The Story of the Young Edgar Cayce*. New York: Morrow, 1974.

SUGRUE, THOMAS. *There is a River: The Story of Edgar Cayce*. Virginia Beach, Va.: A.R.E. Press, 1973.

SWANBERG, W. A. *Citizen Hearst*. New York: Bantam Books, 1971.

THOMAS, LOWELL. *Sir Hubert Wilkins: His World of Adventure*. New York: McGraw-Hill, 1961.
The Urantia Book. Chicago: Urantia Foundation, 1955.

WILKINS, SIR HUBERT, and HAROLD SHERMAN. *Thoughts Through Space*. New York: C & R Anthony, 1951.

Wilkins Archives, Byrd Polar Research Center, Ohio State University.

Index

A

A.R.E. (see also 'Association for Research and Enlightenment'), 5, 6, 18, 19, 27, 54, 94, 133, 150
 library, 4, 26
A.R.E. Journal, 150
Adam and Eve, 223
Addams, Jane, 71, 200
Adler, Alfred, 190
Admiral Perry Byrd Polar Research Institute, 86
Agee, Doris, 44
American Association of Clinical Research, 50
American College of Surgeons, 191
American Magazine, 191
American Medical Association, xxiii, 20–23, 41, 113, 114, 119, 140, 191, 198, 205
American Medical Association for the Advancement of Science, 191
American Medical Missionary College, 190
American Psychiatric Association, 191
American Psycho pathological Association, 191
American Society of Clinical Research, xxiii
Analysis of a Revealed Text, the Urantia Book, 219
Antarctica, 83, 84, 85, 207
 policy for naming discoveries, 84
Archaeology, 142–43
Arctic, 37, 72, 83, 183
Arm force, as reference to writing, 53

Association for Research and Enlightenment (see also 'A.R.E.'), 3, 208
Atlantis, 31, **33**

B

Barraff, Carol A., 150
Battle Creek College, 190
Battle Creek Sanitarium, 190
Battle Creek, Michigan, 41, 43, 68, 69, 190, 196
Beazley, Hugh, 61
Birmingham *Age-Herald*, 28
Birth of a Revelation, 95, 138, 219
Blackburn, James, 61
Blackburn, John, 61, 63, 64
Block, Matthew, 25, 126, 219
Book of Life, 157
Boston, Massachusetts, xxiii, 11
Bowling Green, Kentucky, 30, 64, 198, 203
Bro, Harmon Hartzell, 18
 witnessed Cayce readings, 11
Bromley, Charles 'Bud', 31, 219
Bryant, Charles R., 64
Bunker, Milton N.
 and Nola Smith, 7

C

California, xxiii, 74, 213
Cartwright, Fred, 61
Casey Channel, 83, 207
Cayce, Edgar, xxiv, **2**, 3, 5, 27, 28, 30, 37, 42, 49, 50, 95, 141, 145, 153
 and *Mind at Mischief*, 6
 and Mrs. 3316, 214
 and pin-sticking incident, 50, 63, 77, 199
 and Sherman, 212

and the Institute in Chicago, 68,
    69, 107, 108, 193, 195
death, 48
documentation of readings, 18
education, 11
giving demonstrations, 21
in Chicago, 20, 28, 45, 48, 69,
    108, 206, 207
language during trance, 11–16
marriage to Gertrude Evans,
    145
never remembered, 9, 51
never told, 9
recommends books in trance, 25
source of information, 28, 51,
    54, 56, 144, 152, 159, 205
writing in trance, 99
Cayce, Edgar Evans, 3, 9, **17**, 18,
    20, 144, 210
Cayce, Gertrude Evans, 76, 150,
    197, 198
Cayce, Hugh Lynn, 4, **17**, 18, 51,
    94, 200, 211
    and Sherman, 120, 212, 215,
    216
    writes about *The Urantia Book*,
    94
Celestial visitors, 54
Cerminara, Gina, 14, 48, 57, 58
Challenge to ask more significant
    questions, 22, 174
    Bill Sadler, Jr.'s account, 104,
    132, 133
    Sadler's account, 104, 108, 113
    the Cayce readings, 104, 108,
    133, 207
Chautauqua (see also 'Lyceum'), 41,
    61, 65, 71, 114, 191, 196, 198,
    200, 201, 202, 203, 204, 206,
    214
Chautauqua Express, **60**, 61
Chautauqua Talent magazine, 203
Chicago *Examiner*, xxiv, 67, 68
Chicago Institute of Research and
    Diagnosis, xxiii, 42, 44, 89,
    190, 201
Chicago Medical Mission, 190, 197
Chicago Medical Society, 191

Chicago, Illinois, xxiii, 5, 27, 41, 42,
    68, 71, 75, 113, 130, 140, 219
    articles about Cayce, 67
    as site for Cayce hospital, 20,
    21
Christensen, Emma 'Christy', 16,
    39, 140, 182, 191
Churchward, James, 223
Cincinnati *Times-Star*, xxiv
Circuit (of ascension), 157
Columbus Hospital, 190
Communications (see also 'Quality
    of the communications', and
    'Consistency of messages'), 53,
    55, 58, 74, 104, 115, 133, 173,
    180, 181
Complete Edgar Cayce Readings on
    CD-ROM, 44, 48, 154
Concentric circles, 31, 32, 222
    Abred, 33
    Ceugant, 33
    Gwynfyd, 33
Consistency of messages, 57, 58
Contact Commissioners, 101, 115,
    140, 167, 173, 180, 182
Cooper Medical College, 190
Cosmopolitan magazine, 73, 211
Coverdale, Keith, 64

D

Davis, Gladys (see 'Turner, Gladys
    Davis'), 150
Delucalion, 223
Diversey Arms Hotel, 87
Diversey Parkway, 5, 114
Duke University, 210, 211, 214,
    217

E

E.Q.B. Literary Club, 61, 64, 65
Edgar Cayce on ESP, 44
*Edgar Cayce on Religion and
    Psychic Experience*, 155, 156
*Edgar Cayce, Mystery Man of
    Miracles*, 63
*Edgar Cayce's Photographic
    Legacy*, 30

Edgar Cayce's Story of Jesus, 53, 130
Editorial suggestions
  and Cayce, 117
  and Sleeping Subject, 117
Egyptian, 31
Elliott, Berkeley, 125, 134, 137
ESP, 155, 211
Eugene Field Society, 67, 191

F

Field, Charles Kellogg, 68
Field, Eugene, 67
Field, Roswell, 37, 67, 68, 84, 201
Flood, biblical, 222, 223
Fohi
  Chinese version of Noah, 223
Fort Wayne, Indiana, 141, 196
Forum, 4, 20, 21, 22, 38, 39, 75, 81, 92, 95, 102, 104, 126, 130, 132, 133, 136, 137, 159, 171–73, 183, 206, 212, 213, 215, 216
  becomes a closed group, 113, 173
  beginning, 153, 171
  last meeting, 115, 173
  signs pledges of secrecy, 114, 115
Free will, 157
Freud, Sigmund, 190
Frisch, Dr., 21, 113
Funk, Jesse, 64
Furst, Jeffrey, 53, 57

G

Garden of Eden, 223
Gardner, Martin, 95, 145, 219
Garrett, Eileen, 210, 215
  and Dr. Rhine, 215
  and Sherman, 215
Gault, Robert H., 128
Germain, Walter D., 73
Gods (multiple), 157
Goresline, Dr., 217
Gorgas Memorial Institute in Tropical and Preventive Medicine, 191

Gospels, 159
Great Revelation Book, 74
Grierson, John, 81, 85, 94, 124
Guardian of destiny, 52

H

Hammerschmidt, Judge, 141
Handwriting, 110, 114, 138
  Bill Sadler, Jr.'s comments, 218
  Sadler's comments, 218
Harp, Jesus played the, 153, 209, 210
Harrison, Harry P., 202, 204, 214
Hearst Land, 83, 86, 207
Hearst, William Randolph, 37, 38, 39, **66**
  and Cayce, 48, 67, 68, 83, 201, 202
  and Houdini, 91
  and Sadler, 67, 207
  and Wilkins, 83, 86, 207, 210
  death, 216
History of the Urantia Movement, 22, 99–143, 165–89
Hollywood, California, 74, 212
Hopkinsville Literary Club, 63
Hopkinsville, Kentucky, 42, 60, 61, 63, 69, 196, 198, 201, 203
Hotel Great Northern, 195
Houdini, A Magician Among The Spirits, 91
Houdini, Harry, 37, 38, 39, 89–93, 129, 204, 205, 206, 209
  and Cayce, 206
  and Sadler, 89, 206, 213
  in Chicago, 92, 206
  psychic investigation, 20, 205
How to Know What to Believe, 95, 218
Hull House, 71, 73, 200
Humor, 144
Humor From the Psychic, 144
Hypnosis, 55, 100, 167
  and E.Q.B. meeting, 62, 63
  used on Sleeping Subject, 68, 89

I

ia' suffix, 14, 222
Identity of sleeping subject, 9, 20,
    48, 119, 121, 139, 176, 181
Illinois Psychiatric Association,
    191
Illinois Society for Mental
    Hygiene, Chicago, 191
Illinois State Medical Society, 191
Illinois State Police, 71, 197
Institute of Physiologic
    Therapeutics, 200
International Lyceum Association,
    86, 91, 202, 203
International Lyceum Bureau, 71
International Mark Twain Society,
    41, 191
IPSAB, 150

J

Jeans, James, 25, 26
Jericho, 143
Jesus
    mortal remains, 162
Johnson, Tom, 150

K

Kagan, Bud, 219
Kantor, David, 125
Kellogg Institute, 43
Kellogg Sanitarium, 41, 69
Kellogg, Anna, 39, 140
Kellogg, Ester Smith, 67
Kellogg, John Harvey, 41, 68, 69,
    71, 197, 198, 200
Kellogg, Julia Ann, 68
Kellogg, Lena (see 'Sadler, Lena
    Kellogg'), 39, 41, 68, 107, 197
Kellogg, Moses Smith, 68
Kellogg, Wilfred, 37, 39, 137, 140,
    145, 146, 182, 203, 204
    death, 217
Kentucky Educational Society,
    196

Ketchum, Wesley H., xxiii, 11, 50,
    52, 201
Kulieke, Mark, 95, 114, 128, 144,
    199, 219

L

L&N Railroad, 42
Ladies Home Journal, 191
language
    during contact sessions, 11–16
    Latin, 12, 14
    limitations of, 122, 134, 135,
        155, 176, 217
    of the Cayce readings, 11, 14
    translations of *The Urantia
        Book*, 182
LaSalle Hotel, 193, 194
Latin, 12, 13, 14, 222
Layne, Al, 49, 63, 197
League of Nations, 159
Leary, David M., 30
Light and Life, 155
Lincoln, Abraham, 163
London, England, 83
Loose, Harry
    and Sherman, 74
Loose, Harry J., 37, 38, 197, 199,
    200, 204, 212
    and Sadler, 117
    and Sherman, 95, 212, 213, 214
    death, 214
Lucifer Rebellion, 169
Lyceum (see also 'Chautauqua'), 41,
    202, 203

M

Mandate limiting revealed
    knowledge, 123, 149
Many Mansions, 48
Marion *Chronicle*, 71, 204
Marion, Indiana, 71, 204
Mary Magdalene, 162
McCormick Theological
    Seminary, 190, 208
Melchizedek, 139, 153
Meredith, George, 62
Mesopotamian cities, 31, 220

Metaphysical readings, 153, 204
Meussling, Vonne, Ph.D., 71, 226
Michael, name for Jesus, 161, 169, 170, 175
Millard, Joseph, 63
Mind at Mischief, xxiii, 6, 23, 43, 44–59, 67, 94, 108, 128, 191, 207, 208
  and Hugh Lynn Cayce, 95
Montgomery Park, Califormia, 212
Monticello Hotel, 86
Moody Bible Institute, 197
Moody, Dwight L., 197
Morning Stars sang together, 157
Morontia Life, 88
Mrs. 3316 (Forum member), 4, 37, 38, 39, 94, 214, 215, 216
Mu, 223
Munsterberg, Hugo, 51
Murphy, Dr., 210

N

Nashville, Tennessee, 51
National Association of Authors and Journalists, 191
National Geographic Society (Australia), 85
National Society of Homeopathic Physicians, xxiii
New York, 30, 41, 72, 201, 202, 215
New York stock exchange, 30
New York *Times*, xxiii, xxiv, 11, 201, 202
Night sessions, 45, 48, 52, 104, 145, 170
Noah, 223
Noe, Mr., 48
Norfolk, Virginia, 5, 86, 205, 207
North American Newspaper Alliance, 83
Northwestern University, 128

O

Oregon *Sunday Journal*, xxiv
Origin and Destiny of Man, The, 158

Ouija board, 53, 100

P

Pearl Harbor, 212, 213
Pins, sticking subject with, 50, 63, 76, 77, 199
Pit, Board of Trade game, 30, 76, 198
Plato, 31
Pluto, 222
Poseidon, 31
Post Graduate Medical Center, Chicago, 190
Principles of Nature, Her Divine Revelations, and a Voice to Mankind, 26, 222

Q

Q.K. Kellogg Foundation, Battle Creek, Michigan, 190
Quality of the communications, 57, 58
Quebec, Canada, 27

R

Radio program (Harold Sherman & Hugh Lynn Cayce), 120
Readings
  at night, 48
  consistant, 57, 58
  differences in quality, 58
  humor, 144
  language of, 14, 122, 150
  missing, 19, 27
  Positive manner, 45
Reardon, Fred, 61
Redpath Lyceum and Chautauqua Bureau (see also 'Chautauqua'), 41, 196, 202, 204
Redpath, James, 196
Reincarnation vs. resurrection, xxv, 154, 157, 222, 223
Respiration, during trance, 49, 75, 77
Rheaume, Jacques, 27

Rhine, Dr. J.B., 210, 211
    and Eileen Garrett, 215
    and Sherman, 217
    and Wilkins, 214
Ross, Winston, 87, 94

S

Sacred promise, Sadler's, 47
Sadler, Bill, Jr., 9, 38, 86, 104, 111,
    114, 125, 140, 182, 191, 200,
    218, 219
    and Wilkins, 216
    contributor to *The Urantia
        Book*, 219
    Taped interview, 125
    Transcript of taped interview,
        125–43
Sadler, John Madison, 190
Sadler, Lena Kellogg, 39, 41, 68,
    107, 197
Sadler, Mary (Wharton), 190
Sadler, Samuel Cavins, 190
Sadler, Sarah Isabella (Wilson),
    190
Sadler, William Cavins, 190
Sadler, William Samuel, 16, 27, 30,
    38, 41–43, 46, 68, 71, 81, 91,
    92, 94, 95, 129, 133, 138, 144,
    150, 167, 189, 190–91, 204, 206
    and Eugene Field Society, 67
    and Sherman, 95, 109, 145
    and the AMA, 113, 114
    and the Kelloggs, 67, 68
    and the sleeping subject, 110
    and Wilkins, 12, 81, 83, 207
    Chautauqua lecturer, 113, 206
    professional ethics, 20
    psychic investigation, xxiii, 20,
        42, 107
    sacred promise, 48
    secrecy, xxv
Sadler, Willis Kellogg, 191
Safety deposit box story, 144
Saginaw Police Force, 73
Saginaw, Michigan, 73
Sanskrit, 223
Scottavarata, 223

Seances, 28, 52, 100, 167
Seattle *Times*, xxiv
Secrecy, xxv, 51, 81, 107, 113, 114,
    115, 119, 121, 140, 172, 173,
    175, 206
Seventh Day Adventists, 197
Seventy, The, 181
Sherman, Harold M., 37, 38, 39, **78**,
    81, 86, 199, 204, 211, 218
    and Cayce, 211, 212
    and Chicago, 213, 214
    and Dr. Rhine, 217
    and Eileen Garrettt, 215
    and Hugh Lynn Cayce, 95, 120,
        212, 215, 216
    and Loose, 74, 95, 212, 213,
        214
    and Sadler, 95, 109, 159, 212,
        213, 218
    and Warner Brothers, 74
    and Wilkins, 72, 81, 116, 212,
        215, 216, 217
    death, 219
    Forum member, 212
    in Chicago, 212
Sherman, Martha, 74, 109
Silvi, John
    and Nola Smith, 7
Sir Hubert Wilkins Foundation, 85
*Sir Hubert Wilkins, Enigma of
    Exploration*, 81, 94, 217
Smith, Nola
    and Bill Sadler, Jr., 39
    and Dr. William Sadler, 8, 39
    and Sleeping Subject, 8
    and the A.R.E., 6, 39
Society for Personality Study,
    191
Sources of information, 24, 25, 26,
    29, 52, 54, 57, 58, 82, 93, 104,
    116, 123, 124, 127, 137, 151,
    152, 205, 209, 217, 219
Spencer, Indiana, 190, 196
Spiritual Fellowship Journal, 24,
    25, 123
Spirituality vs. spiritualism, 28, 45,
    47, 52, 100, 131, 167, 202, 204
Spoken messages, 11, 27, 50, 53, 56,
    87, 110, 114, 126, 138

Springfield, Illinois, 71
Sprunger, Meredith J., 114, 141
Stearn, Jess, 63, 65
Stenographer, 49, 87, 110, 111, 112, 114, 115, 132, 133, 134, 135, 138, 150
Stock broker, stories of contact person being, 145
Stock market, 30, 75, 76, 129, 130, 198
Student visitors, 53
Sugrue, Thomas, 30, 49, 51, 62, 65, 79
Sumerian, 31, 219
Swedenborg, Emmanual
    mentioned in *The Principles of Nature, Her Divine Revelations, and a Voice to Mankind*, 223

T

There is a River, the Story of Edgar Cayce, 27, 30, 49, 51, 52, 118, 151, 214
Thomas, Lowell, 86, 94
Thought Adjuster or Spark of God, 52, 140, 150, 168, 177, 217
Thoughts Through Space, 72
Thurston, Howard, xxiii, 37, 89, **90**, 91, 128, 204, 210
    and Sadler, 89, 206
    psychic investigation, 20
Truth About Spiritualism, The, 129
Turner, Gladys Davis, 18, 150
Twain, Mark, 41, 74, 75

U

Universe Around Us, The, 26
University of Illinois, 204
University of Ottawa, 27
Urantia Book, xxiv, 3, 4, 9, 10, 12, 13, 14, 16, 20, 22, 24, 26, 31, 37, 43, 48, 52, 55, 57, 83, 86, 87, 94, 95, 119, 121, 122, 123, 124, 125, 126, 136, 137, 144, 145, 146, 149, 151, 153, 154, 157, 174, 175, 176, 179, 180, 181, 182, 183, 185, 186, 187, 188, 189, 209, 215, 216, 217, 218, 219, 220
    and Hugh Lynn Cayce, 95
    language of, 11–16
Urantia Brotherhood, 3, 5, 94, 137, 181, 183, 184, 185, 186, 187, 216
Urantia Foundation, 9, 81, 136, 137, 182, 185
    and Hugh Lynn Cayce, 95
*Urantia Papers (*see also *'Urantia Book')*, xxv, 3, 4, 16, 44, 49, 79, 83, 92, 95, 100, 101, 104, 107, 109, 111, 116, 119, 122, 125, 133, 135, 145, 167, 169, 172, 173, 175, 176, 177, 180, 181, 213, 216, 217
    reception of, 111
Urantia, the Great Cult Mystery, 95, 145, 219

V

Venture Inward, 94, 95
Virginia Beach, Virginia, 4, 9, 206

W

Warner Brothers
    and Sherman, 74
Washington Hotel, 193, 194
What and Why, 7
White, Ellen, 47
Wilkins archives, 86
Wilkins Foundation (see 'Sir Hubert Wilkins Foundation'), 85
Wilkins, Sir George Hubert, 37, 38, 39, **80**, 111, 114, 127, 132, 138, 140, 183, 200, 201, 207, 209, 210, 211, 214
    amd Sherman, 216
    and Bill Sadler, Jr., 216
    and Dr. Rhine, 214
    and Hearst, 83, 86
    and Hugh Lynn Cayce, 95
    and Sadler, 81, 83, 207
    and Sherman, 72, 73, 75, 81, 116, 212, 215, 217

and the Forum, 215
and the sleeping subject, 23,
    110, 217
and *The Urantia Book*, 12, 37,
    85, 123, 214, 215, 216,
    217, 218
and William W. Kellogg, 212
Antarctic discoveries, 83
death, 94, 217
in Chicago, 87, 208, 212, 217
in Norfolk, VA, 86, 207
knighted, 83
letter to Winston Ross, 87, 94
Lyceum member, 86
poem (his epitaph), 124
Wilkins, Suzanne, 94

World War II, 212
Written messages, 27, 49, 53, 56,
    91, 99, 103, 110, 114, 115, 119,
    126, 127, 133, 134, 138, 145,
    159, 173, 180, 181, 205, 209

X

Xisuthrus, 223

Z

Zend Vest of Zoraster, 223
Zodiac, 32

New for *2023*!
From Bunker Pressler Books

JOHN PENIEL AND THE NEW ORDER OF THINGS
Astronomy, Dendera Zodiac, Calendar, New Year, Mythology, Law of One, John Peniel, Winged Disk, Pyramid Texts, Hepzefa Contracts, Coffin Texts, Atlantis, Legend of Horus, Shabaka Stone, Edgar Cayce, Palermo Stone

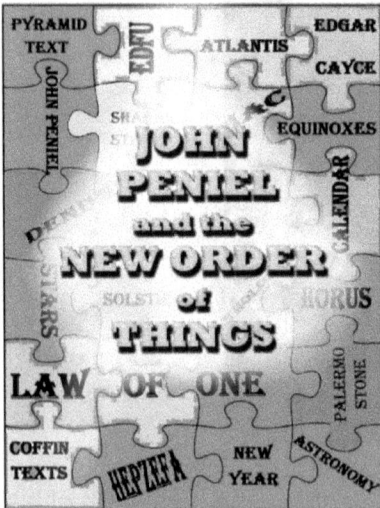

This book corrects many of the erroneous ideas concerning ancient Egyptian texts and beliefs, clarifying that there is a unity of ideas that all point to astronomy as their source. When we remove the mythological and religious ambiguity from our understanding of the texts, it is easy to see the astral nature of their basis. This is important because it helps us to understand the origin of religious belief systems in our world and this under-standing enables us to synchronize material reality with its mental and spiritual essence

ISBN-13 : 978-1732579286

SECRETS IN THE STARS OF ANCIENT EGYPT

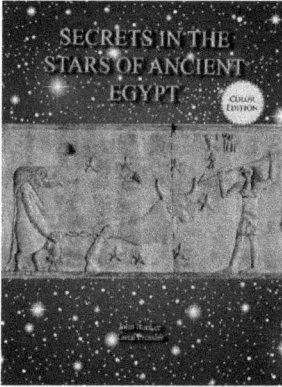

Once in a while a book comes along that changes the way we see history. It provides a new perspective and challenges former beliefs. It breaks the mold of preconceived ideas and opens new vistas - even to generations yet unborn. This is such a book! At last something you can rely on and be sure of! These are the secrets in the stars of Ancient Egypt - the hidden truth of the mythology and the astronomy, and the correct understanding of the mystical and mysterious secrets hidden in the stars of ancient Egypt. The content is the result of decades of original research and translation, combined with an in-depth study of historical astronomy, to reveal important aspects of ancient thought and history that have been an enigma for millennia. The simple truth is no one has ever identified the star constellations in the tomb of Seti I. Likewise, a meaningful commentary on the square zodiac images on the ceiling of the temple of Hathor at Dendera has not been available until now. In addition, the truth behind the misunderstood legend of the death of Osiris is revealed. Finally, there is a comprehensive translation of the inscribed text of the Inventory Stela found at Giza in 1858 by Mariette. These discoveries and more are revealed in *The Secrets in the Stars of Ancient Egypt*, and the historical breakthroughs gained through their understanding are profound and important. Here is a collection of information that focuses on correcting misconceptions about Ancient Egypt, setting the record straight with proof and explanation. It is really an eye opener, and probably will upset the proverbial apple cart!

ISBN-13: 978-1-7325792-1-7 (Black & White edition)
ISBN-13: 978-1-7325792-3-1 (Color edition)

EDGAR CAYCE'S SPHINX, THE HALL OF RECORDS & THE HOLY GRAIL

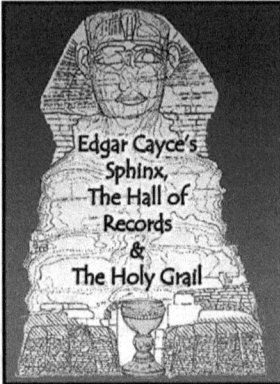

A condensed yet thorough revelation of the exact location of the Hall of Records that Edgar Cayce predicted would be found. This book is a cohesive masterpiece that connects the fragmented bits of information scattered throughout dozens of readings given over a period of many years by Edgar Cayce. You won't be disappointed with this dramatic evidence! The quest for the Hall of Records has become tantamount to the quest of the Holy Grail.

ISBN-13: 978-1732579224

"THE SPHINX AND THE LOST HALL OF RECORDS"
LECTURE GIVEN AT THE HOUSTON A.R.E. CENTER, JANUARY 17, 2015

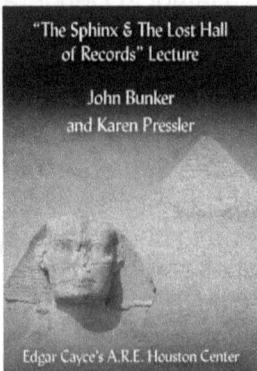

This is the complete PowerPoint presentation given at the Houston Edgar Cayce Center in January 2015, complete with lecture transcript. It includes all of the reasoning and proof for the conten-tion that there really is a connection between the Sphinx and the location of the Hall of Records, but current efforts have been guided by a misunderstanding of the clues.

ISBN-13: 978-0988500105

THE COFFIN TEXTS RESURRECTED
AN ENGLISH TRANSLATION WITH HIEROGLYPHIC TEXT

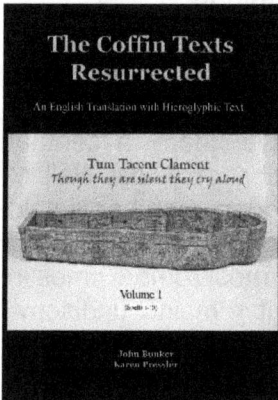

The Coffin Texts
Resurrected

An English Translation with Hieroglyphic Text

Tum Tacent Clament
Through they are silent they cry aloud

Volume 1
(Spells 1-3)

John Bunker
Karen Pressler

This volume shows the hieroglyphic text and English translation of each of the first ten spells from The Egyptian Coffin Texts 1: Texts of Spells 1-75 by Adriaan De Buck, published by the Oriental Institute and Chicago University Press in 1935. In 1973, nearly 4 decades later, R. O. Faulkner published the first volume of a three volume summary translation of spells 1 to 1185. Now we have begun to take a fresh look at the coffin texts with this translation and commentary, which includes the historical background of the coffin texts as told by James Henry Breasted. The introductory material includes a history of the Egyptian calendar that suggests its beginning may date to the 11th millennium B.C.E., and commentary on the Pyramid Texts, the Coffin Texts, Book of the Dead, and how some of the ideas from these ancient texts have been preserved in the Holy Bible.

ISBN-13: 978-0988500198

EDGAR CAYCE AND THE HALL OF RECORDS

Solving the Mystery of the Hall of Records and the Sphinx Connection Using Ancient Egyptian Texts, Astronomy, and the Edgar Cayce Readings

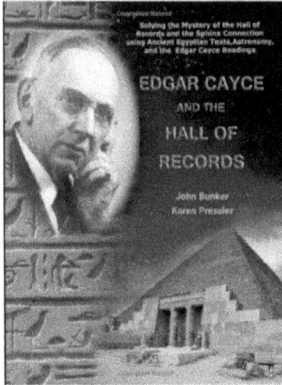

The famous psychic and healer, Edgar Cayce, was providing clues in the "life readings" he gave nearly a century ago to the location of a lost Hall of Records. This hidden chamber is said to contain historical archives and artifacts from the most remote times in prehistory. Yet, it remains undiscovered. Most people have assumed that it will be found in a chamber under the Sphinx at Giza, but all attempts to locate it there have met with failure. At last the evidence has been reevaluated outside of the traditional thinking, to reveal incredible new conclusions that are difficult to argue. The sphinx that guards the Hall of Records is not the Giza Sphinx at all, but rather a sphinx star constellation in the night sky. And the Hall of Records is not below the ground, but rather elevated up among the stars at the top of the great middle pyramid at Giza. Finally, we can point directly to a spot and say with confidence, "This is where the Hall of Records will be found." The facts are irrefutable!

ISBN-13: 978-0966977486

THE BOOK OF AKER

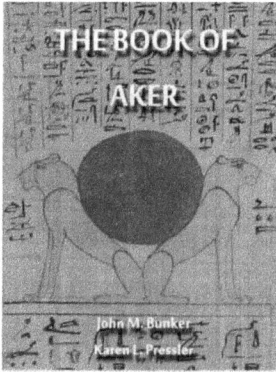

A complete new translation of the *Book of Aker,* illustrated with 214 black and white illustrations and 170 color illustrations. This is the first time an exhaustive translation of the complete Book of Aker from the tomb of *Ramesses VI* has ever been done. It includes detailed images from the tomb, the com-plete hieroglyphic texts with word by word translations, and explanations throughout. This is intended for serious students of ancient Egyptian texts and ideas.

ISBN-13: 978-0966977431

THE ABRIDGEMENT OF THE BOOK OF AM TUAT

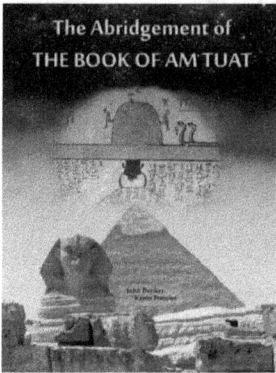

It has become clear that the tomb of *Osiris* and the Hall of Records will be found in the upper section of the Pyramid known as *Khafre's.* The evidence is overwhelming with this fresh translation of the *Am Tuat* in an astronomical context. Include-ing more analysis, illustration, and supplemental material than ever before, Bunker and Pressler prove that the middle Giza pyramid is much older than previously thought, and exhibits evidence of two entirely different civilizations, hundreds of thousands of years apart. With this groundbreaking research, a new level of understanding humanity's history has begun.

ISBN-13: 978-0966977479

ENGLISH TRANSLATIONS OF THE MASTERS
BY BUNKER PRESSLER BOOKS

A FRAGMENT OF ANCIENT EGYPTIAN ANNALS (ENGLISH TRANSLATION OF EIN BRUCHSTÜCK ALTÄGYPTISCHER ANNALEN):
An English Translation of a 1902 Presentation about the Palermo Stone by Dr. Heinrich Schäfer

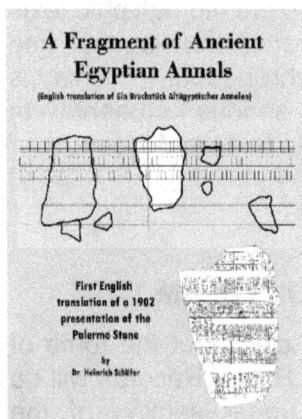

A Fragment of Ancient Egyptian Annals

(English translation of Ein Bruchstück Altägyptischer Annalen)

First English translation of a 1902 presentation of the Palermo Stone

by Dr. Heinrich Schäfer

In 1901 three of Egyptology's early pioneers Dr. Kurt Sethe, and Dr. Ludwig Borchardt collaborated in a discussion and study of a fragment of stone that came to be known as the Palermo Stone, because its home was the museum of Palermo, Italy where it was first displayed in 1877. Schäfer prepared a preliminary report of their efforts that was presented at the General Session on March 6, 1902.

ISBN-13: 978-8986357119

THE PALERMO STONE (Edouard Naville)

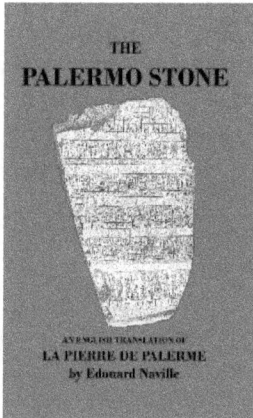

The Palermo Stone is one of the earliest known records of Egyptian history, being a fragment of the Royal Annals, which the Egyptians used to record their most significant historical events annually over the course of many years. One of the first studies of the Palermo Stone was made by Edouard Naville, entitled *La Pierre de Palerme,* published in French in 1903 in a journal of works related to Egyptian and Assyrian philology and arche-ology. Now, it is again brought to the forefront with the first English edition of this original study.

ISBN-13: 979-8-986357102

THE TEMPLE PLANS OF DENDERA (Johannes Dümichen)

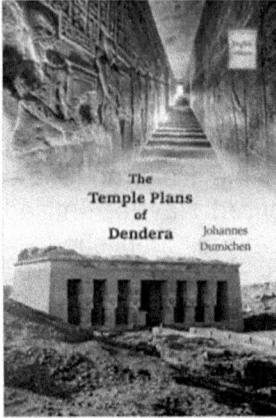

This book, the first English translation of Johannes Dümichen's critical 1865 work *Bauurkunde der Tempelangen von Dendera*, further opens the discoveries of the original Egypt-ologists to the English-speaking world. It contains an extensive study of the Hathor Temple at Dendera, previously neglected by other Egyptologists, and particularly a document found preserved in a cavity in the temple wall, which described the restoration carried out by King Khufu of the fourth dynasty. Dümichen's study reveals multiple restorations to the building over a long period of time by various Egyptian kings, and suggests Dendera may date from the time of the Followers of Horus near the dawn of Egyptian civilization.

ISBN-13: 978-1732579248

BRUGSCH'S 1883 THESAURUS (VOLUME I): FIRST ENGLISH TRANSLATION

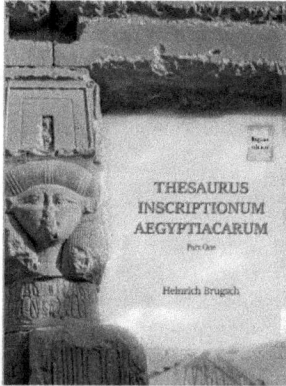

This is the only English translation ever made of Heinrich Brugsch's *Thesaurus* on ancient Egyptian astronomy and astrology. Originally published in handwritten German script in 1883, it was the most in-depth study ever made of the temple of Hathor at Dendera and includes Brugsch's abundant illustrations. Now for the first time it is available to the English-speaking world. It includes Egyptian hieroglyphics, along with a smattering of Greek, Coptic and Latin and several notes from the translators. Over a century has passed since it was first published. This English translation has been motivated by the need for wider access to the works of the original pioneers of Egyptology. Heinrich Brugsch was a leading expert of ancient Egyptian studies who lived during the years of the great masters and fathers of Egyptology and dedicated his life to the pursuit of knowledge and understanding of the greatest civilization on earth.

ISBN-13: 978-1732579279

www.ingramcontent.com/pod-product-compliance
Lightning Source LLC
Chambersburg PA
CBHW062204270326
41930CB00009B/1647